ASSET CLASS MASTERY

Maximize Profits From Forex, Futures, and Cryptos

WAYNE WALKER

TABLE OF CONTENTS

INTRODUCTION

Congratulations on your personal copy of *Asset Class Mastery.* This unique book will provide you with a foundation of the techniques required for profiting from forex, futures, and cryptocurrencies. You will journey across several asset classes to acquire a broad and personal understanding of the capital and cryptocurrency markets. The emphasis throughout is on practical applications. Thanks for choosing this book!

CHAPTER 1:
What is Forex?

In this chapter we will examine the foreign exchange market, the participants, what makes the market move, and why you should want to trade it.

So what is Forex (Foreign Exchange) or FX as many people call it? , it is the world's most liquid market. The average daily turnover is over 4 trillion US Dollars. This is a huge number, but to put it in perspective, one day of FX is roughly 2 to 3 months of trading volume on the New York Stock Exchange. This is powerful, it means a lot of liquidity and that a lot of people are involved in it.

It is OTC traded, meaning over-the-counter with no central exchange, in contrast to the equity or commodity markets where there are central exchanges that buyers and sellers meet. With FX, it is just you and your broker/dealer.

It is open for 24/5 trading, from Sydney 5 AM on Mondays to New York 5 PM on Fridays. Plenty of time, allowing for round the clock trading.

Centers and Participants

Who are the people that are involved in this FX phenomenon?

First we will take a look at the FX centers. The main centers of FX are the UK, US and Japan. They are responsible for the bulk of the trading. Australia, Singapore and Switzerland are also important players in the market, but the main players remain US, UK and Japan.

Banks and Financial Institutions

It is primarily major banks and financial institutions, they account for roughly 50% of the transactions. They trade electronically amongst themselves.

The central banks are also involved and their role is to intervene in an attempt to influence the value of their currencies.

Let us take a closer look at this. Maybe the most famous of central banks, the Federal Reserve Board, they and also the Bank of Japan, are at times known to be active participants in the market in an attempt to influence the strength or weakness of their currencies. A FX trader must be aware of the roles that they play.

Additional Participants

There are now FX hedge funds, years ago if you mentioned FX hedge funds most people would not know what you were talking about, because they did not exist. There are funds that trade either one particular currency or regional currencies, and for those that have an interest they are available.

Other participants are the brokers, both voice and electronic, they serve as intermediaries between banks and dealers. Banks and dealers turn to them for assistance in finding the best deals, but the days of voice brokers are numbered, because most activity now is electronic. There are many firms today that have dealer free desks.

Corporations are also involved, especially the multinationals who have currency risk that needs to be hedged and also for their own speculation. Several international corporations have their own trading desks which they use for prop or proprietary trading.

A hedging example could be, an American company purchases goods from Japan and they receive an invoice that will be due in Yens. To hedge against a potential loss, where the amount due might increase in USD due to fluctuations in the currency, they open a position in the market.

A note on hedging, what we are discussing is removing the risk of holding a particular asset. The main focus is not necessarily on making a profit. For example, in the futures market we might have a wheat farmer and he is what we would say, long wheat. He is afraid of a price fall, so he sells wheat futures contracts to be hedged in case of a fall. If prices do fall, he would make up the loss on the down side. He does not make a profit, but he does remove the risk of holding the wheat.

Private Purposes

For most of us, international travel is a common activity, therefore most people when travelling will need the currency of their destination.

Our overseas purchases are also a factor. If you are sitting in New York and are looking to buy a pair of shoes in London over the internet, normally they will not accept USD, so you will need to convert to British Pounds.

There is also speculation, and this has been one of the main drivers in turning FX into a very hot market over the past few years where people are buying and selling just for speculative purposes.

What moves FX?

What is going on in the market? Why does it move? Several things, it could be rumors , it could be from government intervention, for example if the Bank of Japan enters the market in an attempt to shore up the Yen to prevent a slide, some traders might take it as a cue to start being long (buying) Yens and short (selling) the other crosses against it.

Data

Non-farm payroll is one of the major reports. Also whenever there is a rate decision from the Fed, Bank of England, ECB, or Bank of Japan etc., these are known market movers.

Wars, terrorist acts, whether it is events in the Middle East or other hot spots in the world, they can and do affect the market and in some cases quite drastically.

Central banks, as we touched on with their intervention, sometimes will do as we say "talk down" a currency. For example, bank governors without entering the market with direct intervention can influence it. It could be something where a central bank governor passes a remark at a news conference saying "I think the currency is getting overvalued and we might need to do something about it" or in some cases they might say "the strength of the currency is of concern to us and it's affecting our competitiveness." Depending on who is saying it, the results can be dramatic, and in some cases it is due to a total misunderstanding of what the person was trying to say.

Other Events

Political events and elections can also be major influencers. Someone who has a hawkish view of their currency, being elected to office could be a signal that the currency will appreciate.

Technical levels are also important with some currencies, especially with the round numbers that traders like to focus on. An example could be of a currency pair that is trading at 1.3995 and it has never been above 1.4000, then it begins moving even closer to 1.4000. This 1.4000 level could be seen as psychological that will be watched very closely, and if it is broken you could see what is called a breakout to the upside.

Using our example, if the currency pair is trading at 1.3995 and it goes above 1.4000, you might see that it shoots up to 1.4095 and then drops all the way back to 1.3995. Then we would say it was a false breakout, but there is the chance that it could be real and remain at the 1.4095 level.

Why do you want to trade FX?

You might be saying to yourself, all this is great info but why should I want to trade FX? There are many reasons.

Liquidity

Number one is liquidity, it is unmatched, there is nothing out there even close, as we mentioned at the beginning just a day of FX is two to three months of volume on the New York Stock Exchange. That is powerful.

24 Hour Trading

You have the 24 hour trading possibility, you can trade night or day. There is nothing else that offers this type of flexibility, and for the majority of traders who are business owners or have full time jobs, in some cases even university students, this is great.

Long or Short Option

FX gives the long or short option, this is very important. Traditionally most people are accustomed to being long, buying a particular share and hoping the share will increase in value. FX gives you the option of going short, it is a different way of looking at the market, but it can be lucrative. For the savvy traders it is a tool to use to take advantage of the market.

Correlation to other asset classes

Low correlation to other asset classes, this is important for those who are trying to have a diversified portfolio. When there is market turmoil, whether it is in commodities, or equities, Forex stands apart. Stocks can take a dive or commodity prices explode but Forex is Forex, it is moved by other forces. FX is not what you want to have as 80% of your portfolio, but having some exposure to FX is a prudent thing.

Basic FX Terms

I might not make you into a super trader overnight but having an understanding of these terms will make it easier to communicate in the FX community and also speak with your trading partners.

Your base currency is your market exposure, and the variable currency is used to calculate your profit and loss (P/ L). Taking a EURUSD example, the EUR is your base currency. Your exposure and your margin calculation will be done in Euro. The profit and loss will be done in USD.

Depending on the base currency of your account, your P/L will be calculated again, so for this example (EURUSD) and if you have Sterling (GBP) as your base currency then the profit and loss from US Dollars would then be converted to your base (GBP).

Basic terms continuing, we have EURUSD at 1.5800, what we are saying is 1 Euro is equivalent to 1.58 Dollars, or that the Euro is stronger than the US Dollar.

The Spread

This is a term that gets tossed around often amongst traders. The spread is the difference between the bid and the ask price. If on the bid the sell price is 1.5800 and the buy ask price is 1.5802, we have a 2 pips difference. We will say the spread is 2 pips.

Long, Short and Square

Long

You are buying,

Short

You are selling.

Examples

If you are long EURUSD or long Euro Dollar as we would say, then you are long Euro and you have sold or short USD. If you are short Euro Dollar, you are short Euros and long Dollars.

Square

You are closed. In clear terms to square a long 500,000 EURUSD position you need to short 500,000 EURUSD to remove your market exposure.

Trader Jargon

This is a little extra that I have included for those of you who will be trading FX regularly.

First is **Cable (GBPUSD)**, a term you will hear repeatedly and it is Great British Pound against the US Dollar.

Swissie is the Swiss Franc (CHF)

Aussie is the Australian Dollar (AUD)

Kiwi is the New Zealand Dollar (NZD)

Loonie is the Canadian Dollar (CAD)

The Figure

Is 00 at the end of a number, so sometimes while trading, you might speak to a dealer and he might say Euro Dollar is at "1.33 the figure" meaning 1.3300.

Stop Out

All your positions have been closed and it is something that you normally do not want to hear.

OCO

One cancels the other, is normally when you have a limit and stop order connected, if one gets filled the other is cancelled.

Filled

You now have the position. For example, you have a 3 way order that has the price level of where you want to enter the market, once that level is reached you are now filled.

A **quarter** is 250,000

A **half** is 500,000

One is one million

As stated, knowing these terms will make it easier to speak with your dealers or trading counterparts. For those thinking of getting into trading for a living then you definitely must know these terms.

FX Trade Calculations

Many people place FX trades, but most do not have an understanding of the things that are behind it. Before anyone gets into FX trading it is important that they are aware of the components in the margin, calculating the P/L, and the rollover principle. Let us review these areas.

Margin Requirements Awareness

At most FX houses traders are trading on margin and are not doing physical FX trading. The physical FX is where 1 dollar equals 1 dollar in value. With margin trading, you can open a 1 million EURUSD position, with a margin requirement of 1% which is 10,000 Euros. Another example, a 10,000 account balance with a 100,000 position would need 1,000 Euros to keep the position open.

Profit and Loss in Pips

Pips are the smallest price change that an exchange rate can make. We use EURUSD as an example, 1.5280 to 1.5281 is a one pip move. We have USDCAD 0.9955 it moves to 0.9956 also a one pip move.

Let us take an example of profit and loss in pips: Buy 100,000 EURUSD at 1.5100 take profit at 1.5160, 60 pips. You have a stop loss at 1.5070, 30 pips, this is from your entry position.

In pip terms we have here what is called a 2 to 1 ratio, when you go long EURUSD at 1.5100, take profit at 1.5160 and a stop loss at 1.5070.

Pip Value

There are several ways to calculate pip value. Since this is reality based guide we will use the simple way. Let us use the EURUSD example, which is quoted with 4 decimal places, ex.

1.5100, and a nominal value (the amount being traded) of 100,000.

First, count the amount of decimal places that you have and in this example it is 4. Starting from the right, remove 4 numbers from the nominal value (100,000) and you will get the value of each pip. Removing 4 zeros, show us that each pip is 10 Dollars. Remember as we covered earlier, the counter currency USD is used to calculate your profit and loss.

Taking it further, a 60 pip profit (60 x 10 USD) gives you 600 USD, or if you had a 30 pip loss (30 x 10) is 300 USD. When you are using ratio trading in your strategy, it must be that your chance of making a profit is greater than the chance of a loss.

Rollovers

This is something that has given FX traders headaches for many years, but it is not a complicated concept. A lot of people skip the rollover in training but we will address it here.

If you are long EURUSD, you are long Euro and short USD. You are holding Euros and you will earn interest on them. You are also borrowing or shorting USD, therefore you pay interest on what you borrow. The difference in interest is either positive or negative which is your swap.

On the reverse, if you are shorting EURUSD you are short Euros and long USD. You are borrowing the Euros in this case and you are now holding US Dollars. The interest difference is either positive or negative which is the swap.

CHAPTER 2:
3 Way Orders

+

Intro to Support and Resistance

The components of a 3 way order

Having satisfied your entry conditions, your initial order would be your entry order, sometimes called the primary order, it is the order used to enter the trade.

Next is your limit order, profit taking order, or as I say the fun order, this is where you are take your profits out of the market.

Finally we have the stop loss order which is used to limit your losses. A traders golden rule "no cash no trading", a stop loss is very important.

What are the advantages of 3 ways?

Remote Trading

3 way orders allow you to do remote trading. This is a great benefit for a lot of people, because most of us are working or running a business and do not have time to sit and watch trades minute by minute. With 3 way orders you can be active in the markets without being tied to your desk or news reports every second of the day.

Discipline

It instills discipline to your trading because the parameters are defined before you enter the trade and this is such an important point that we will revisit it. One thing is noted as the key difference between those who make a profit trading and those who are losing, is having the parameters set before trading.

Institutional traders, people whose profession is trading, they are using variations of these 3 ways orders. Where they will take profit and where they will cut the loss to preserve cash, is decided prior to entering the trade.

Minimizes the emotion of trading

When the parameters are predefined, it does not leave any room for you to interfere and start retooling everything in the middle of the trade. This is crucial.

Ratio Trading

Ratio trading is your risk reward ratio and it is comprised of your entry level, stop loss and a take profit target. Ratio trading also refers to a win/loss ratio either 2 to 1, 3 to 1, etc.

We begin with a hypothetical trade. You have an entry price buying EURODOLLAR at 1.5550, you have a stop loss at 1.5525 which is 25 pips below, then you have a profit target at 1.5600, this is 50 pips. This combination gives you a ratio of 2 to 1.

Looking at a 3 way order with a 3 to 1 ratio, you buy EURUSD at 1.5550, stop loss 1.5525, 25 pips, and here we have a greater profit target 1.5625. The risk reward is 3 to 1.

Intro to Support and Resistance

With support and resistance levels we are getting into the basics of technical analysis. This is not the chapter on technical analysis, the intent is to give you the Practical Technical Analysis that you need to know in order to understand the next chapter on Trading Tactics.

Support Level

The support level is the price at which the instrument being traded has historically had difficulty falling below. Some people call it the floor. What is important to remember with the support level is that it changes along with your time frame. The support level that you see for an hour chart will be different from one that displays a day or a week. Therefore use a support and resistance level that matches your trading time frame.

Resistance Level

The resistance level is the price level where the currency or instrument that you are trading has historically had difficulty trading above.

The chart time frame should match your trading time horizon. A one hour resistance is totally different from a week's or a month's resistance. As with the support level the parameters must match up.

We will explore deeper into technical analysis in the later chapters.

CHAPTER 3:
Trading Tactics

Here we will examine the major reasons why traders lose money and most important we will explore the solutions.

Unrealistic Expectations

It is important when getting into trading, as with many things, one must have a realistic idea of what you are dealing with. Unrealistic expectations can take the form of someone starting with what is sometimes called a mini-trader account of 1,000 or maybe 2,000 USD and expecting overnight riches.

I have even seen where you can even begin with 100 or 200 dollars which is fine. There is nothing wrong with the amount, but those same traders at 100 or 200 dollars are expecting to have 1,000 or 2,000 dollars in their accounts within a few weeks or even in a couple days. There are firms out there who have actually mentioned or even promised them that they can do this. While I am not saying it is impossible, I am saying it is unrealistic. It is essential that you do have a sense of reality to your trading.

No Plan

No plan as we have discussed, would be similar to arriving at an airline counter and saying "give me a ticket", which does not make much sense. With planning, your trading needs to have an alignment of timeframe and the results that you are expecting to receive.

If you like FX then it is a good idea to stick with FX and build a base from there and later explore other instruments. Maybe even begin trading FX futures because once you have a good understanding of FX then you can start looking into offshoots of it, for example in the futures markets.

If you are familiar with trading equities then you might want to explore CFDs (Contracts For Difference) which are equity derivatives. They are traded by active traders. Again it is all working with the plan that you must have to begin.

Too Much Risk

It could be the person with 100 dollars in their account or even 100,000. It is not the amount that is critical, but the amount you are risking in relation to the funds available.

A simple example, if you have 10,000 USD in your account and are trading a 100,000 EURUSD position, each pip is 10 dollars. This is not that much, which is fine depending on your risk profile. If you then switch to trading a 1,000,000 position each pip is now worth 100 dollars. If you have 10,000 USD in your account and you are long, a 10 pip move lower leaves you automatically with a loss of 1,000 dollars.

Confusing Trading With Investing

In my years as a banker, I have had countless clients who I had to again and again point out that they should not confuse the two. Trading is about making money, it is income generating activity. You are moving in and out of trades, unlike investing which is more long term. It could be that some of your investment goals are derived from your trading but do not confuse them.

The instruments that you are trading, for example FX which is active, you are not investing you are trading, and hopefully earning income. Another example could be CFDs.

It might seem basic to some, but speaking from experience of advising clients globally there are still many out there that get trading and investment confused.

Solutions

It's ok to talk about problems and challenges, but obviously we need to have some solutions.

Low Leverage

We discussed the problems with too much risks, the solution is using low leverage. You plan to open a 100,000 dollar position on EURUSD where each pip is worth 10 dollars, if you are not 100% sure of this trade you might want to begin with 50,000. You keep the leverage low because it gives you time to think, to react more effectively, and you are not as sensitive to changes in the market.

Scaling In Scaling Out

Scaling in scaling out is one of my favorites. I use it with investing and also with my trading. Scaling in scaling out, the theory behind it is that you allow the market to tell you which way to go, it is that simple.

An example, I plan to buy 1,000 shares of GCMS after having done my technical and fundamental analysis. How to begin? I would start with a 200 or 250 shares position and allow the market to confirm if I am on the right path. If I bought GCMS shares at 100 dollars and they suddenly jump to 125 per share, great, the marketing is confirming that I made the correct decision. In this example if I began with 200 shares, I would then add another 200 or 250 and repeat the process until I reach my goal of a 1,000 shares.

There are some who might say I missed out a little on the move from 100 to 125 and I did somewhat, but I am also more secure in my decision by being patient. On the reverse, getting back to scaling out, let us say if the market had moved against me, instead of having 1,000 shares at risk initially, it would have been only 200. Obviously there is a trade off, but from experience, it is to the advantage of those who are scaling in scaling out.

Another example, let us say you bought 200 shares at 100 dollars each and the price suddenly drops to 90. What I would suggest, instead of selling everything immediately, that you consider selling only 50 or 75 because the drop could be due to an overreaction in the market. There are several things that could be at play, for example a false rumor, again you are allowing the market to guide you along the correct path. Of course if the price continues to fall then you sell more. Another way to look at it, using the analogy of driving on the highway, if you have a long straightaway you speed up and if you have a lot of curves you slow down, it seems to work.

Trade Liquid Markets

To trade liquid markets is something I can't overemphasize. There are people in the equity market that trade Over the Counter Bulletin Board (OTCBB) or other thinly traded shares and in FX it is exotic currencies (often low liquidity) which is fine, as long as you are aware of the risk. Liquidity is critical especially as a trader, an investor is not as time sensitive, but if you are trading where you do need to make sudden moves you want to be in a liquid market.

Liquid, to be very clear, is the ability to come in and out of the trade with ease. Being in a trade and having paper profits is wonderful, but when it is time to convert the paper profits and if you are unable to do so, then it is a bad joke as you can only watch them, not very nice. On the other side if you are in a loss and are unable to exit that position, it turns into a nightmare. I don't care who is giving tips, or whatever blog you are reading, you must trade liquid markets, there is no other way.

News Trading

This is for the news traders out there and if you are thinking of trading over numbers (when market data is being released) think again.

There are different systems that these traders use to trade over numbers in an attempt to be smarter than the banks, all I can say is that it is a tactic that I would not suggest until you have plenty of market experience.

If you want to trade over numbers, be aware that the price where your order might get filled or executed could be very different from what you had in mind. For those who trade with providers who guarantee pricing, I would wager that 9.99 out of 10 have a clause in the fine print that states the guarantee is only valid under normal market conditions. Meaning that over numbers the price that you see might not be what you will get.

Selecting Currency Pairs

In FX select a few pairs and get to know them like a close friend. A lot of people begin FX by trading the "majors", EURUSD, GBPUSD, USDCAD, USDJPY, or AUDUSD for example. Of the majors, get to know a few of them well whether it is EURSEK/Euro Swedish, for those in the Scandinavian market or EURJPY for those in the rest of Europe.

Personally, I trade only three or four for the most part. After a while once you begin trading these currency pairs they will become familiar and you will get a deeper sense of how they move.

Placing Orders Strategically

You want to be first in line when getting your orders filled, and placing limits orders before the resistance is effective because the resistance levels are known to everyone already. You want to get filled right before it hits resistance if you are a technical trader and at support you either want to be a little above it or a little beneath the support level if long, just to make sure it wasn't a false breakout to the downside.

To conclude, the most successful traders use a system. They have a set entry, exit, position size, and they are going to scale in/out. As we covered at the beginning you must have a plan, it is what separates the professionals from gamblers.

CHAPTER 4:
Selecting a Trading Partner

We will review the important aspects of selecting a trading partner.

What is Important?

Liquidity

Liquidity at all times, especially in periods of volatility as we discussed in previous sections, it is so important that we mention it again. Your trading partner must be able to provide you with it.

It is important for the instruments that you are trading, whether it is FX or shares. FX crosses are liquid but you also need to be with a partner that has access to this liquidity or else you could be in the bad joke situation where you have a profit but are unable to collect.

Fast Execution

Fast execution, so that when you click, you get the indicated price. Liquidity is a key factor in execution speed.

Trustworthy

As with any type of relationship, you want to be with a trading partner that has a good reputation and is known for being trustworthy and has a solid financial base. You do not want to trade with someone that is at risk of collapsing. Getting a recommendation from a trusted friend is encouraged.

Reliable Platform

Your platform needs to be reliable. It is not optimal to have a platform that is often down when you are ready to trade or has lots of technical issues.

When trading during normal market conditions and if you are frequently getting re-quoted prices, that is a red flag.

Access to news and market data

Your platform or trading partner should have access to news or to what is sometimes called streaming news from the different news agencies for ex Reuters, Bloomberg. You also want to get access to their market making desk. If they do not have one, they should be able to provide you with market flow data, for example if traders are currently long EURUSD or there seems to be a movement to USDJPY. This is important, in particular when trading Forex.

Best in class strategy team

No strategy team is perfect, but you do want one that is reliable and that you trust is giving you unbiased market analysis. As with the other topics you want to speak with friends to get their opinions on the recommendations from the strategy teams they deal with.

Reliable Charting System

We have a saying that charts are for "indicative purposes only", they are not the market, yet you want charts that give a good idea of where the market is. Another factor, depending on the charting system, the chart will only reflect the bid (sell price).

In my years of working at a trading desk, I have had numerous discussions with clients after a "bad fill" (trading jargon, for your trade was executed at a price worse than what you expected). In these disputes clients would look at the chart and say "but the chart says this, and this is what I want to get", very important point, the chart is indicative the chart is not the market.

Any broker that you deal with, you want them to trade at where the market is and not the chart. The best words of advice when dealing with a professional dealer or institutional broker over a trade dispute, is that you discuss the market price and stay away from what the chart says. If they are professionals the first thing they will mention to you is where the market was and not where the chart was, because people trade the markets not charts.

How do you find the good guys?

Speak to friends who are trading and of course you may contact me.

CHAPTER 5:
Advanced Technical Analysis For Forex

Introduction

We continue our journey from the foundation forex knowledge that you should now have to acquire a much deeper understanding of technical analysis for forex. The emphasis remains on practical applications. You will be introduced to new strategies along with the know-how on how to apply them. We will also examine advanced technical analysis indicators that can increase your money making ability. The later sections cover advanced *fundamental* analysis and the often overlooked area of trader psychology. These sections are a bonus to traders of all types.

CHAPTER 6:
Charting Essentials

Charts are a forex trader's best tool. As a trader, you will most likely use your charts more than any other available tool. Since your charts will play such a large role in your trading, it is important that you become familiar with them. The more comfortable you are with your charts, the easier it will be to become a profitable forex trader.

To help you become acquainted with charts and how you can effectively use them, we will cover the following concepts: chart setup, chart timeframes, chart types. We will also cover the useful technical indicators you can add to your charts to improve your trading results in the later chapters. We will begin with some base concepts to quickly prep you for more advanced content later.

Chart Setup

Let us start from the base and take a look at how a forex price chart is put together. Once you understand the basics, you will find it easier to apply the more advanced concepts to your technical analysis. Forex price charts are built on two axes: the X axis (horizontal axis) and the Y axis (vertical axis).

The X axis runs horizontally along the bottom of the chart providing a timeline for everything that has happened on the chart. The most recent price action is shown on the right side of the chart.

The Y axis runs vertically along the right side of the chart providing a price scale for the price movement on the chart. Lower prices are shown toward the bottom of the chart and the higher prices are shown toward the top of the chart.

When you combine the two axes together, you can see at what price a currency pair was trading at a particular time in the past.

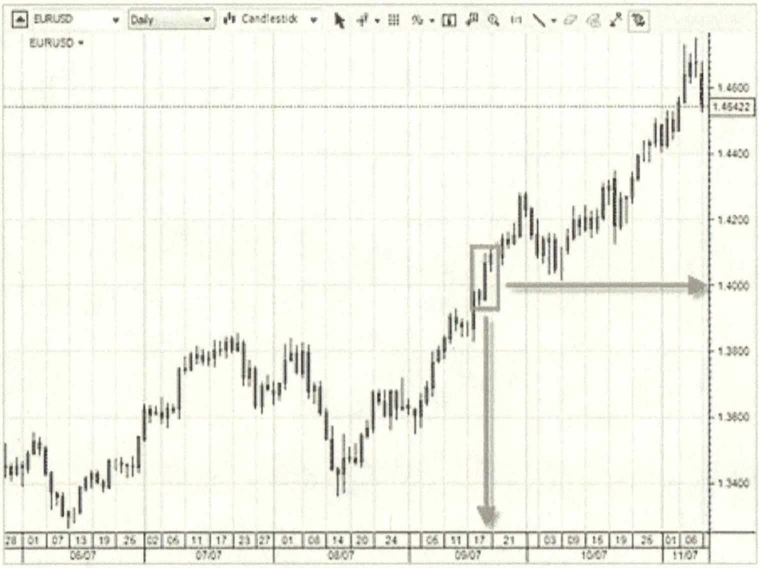

Chart Types

Forex charts give you the ability to analyze the price movement of a currency pair in various formats, from bar charts to candlestick charts. You have the option to select which format is best for you.

Technical analysis is a skill that traders develop, and different traders like to practice their "art" on different types of charts. Some traders believe they can see and analyze support and resistance levels better on a line chart while other traders feel they get more information on price movements on a bar or a candlestick chart. Technical analysts tend to work with the following three chart types:

Line Charts

Line charts are the most basic type of chart. Technical analysts often use line charts to quickly identify support and resistance levels. Line charts only have basic information plotted on them, which means there is not a lot of other information to cloud your analysis. You create a line chart by plotting the closing price of each trading period on a chart and then connecting each closing price with a line. You can see an example of the line chart.

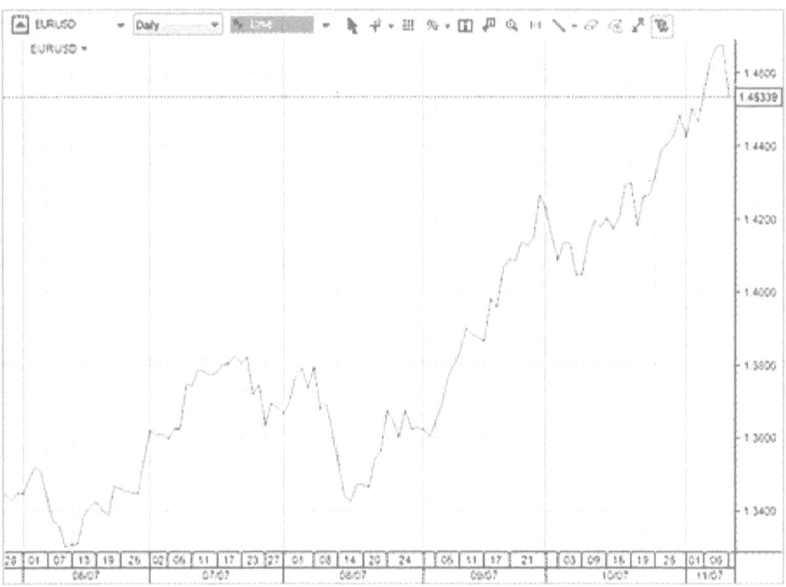

Bar Charts

Bar charts provide more information than a line chart. Technical traders often use bar charts to gain more information about how a currency pair's price fluctuated during each trading period. Whereas line charts only plot the closing price from each trading period, bar charts plot the opening, high, low and closing prices from each period.

You create a bar chart by plotting a series of bars across the chart. Each bar represents one trading period. To create a bar, you plot the high and low price of a trading period and connect them with a vertical line. Next, you plot the opening price out to the left side of the vertical line you have just drawn and connect that point to the vertical line with a horizontal line. Last, you plot the closing price out to the right side of the vertical line you have just drawn and connect that point to the vertical line with a horizontal line.

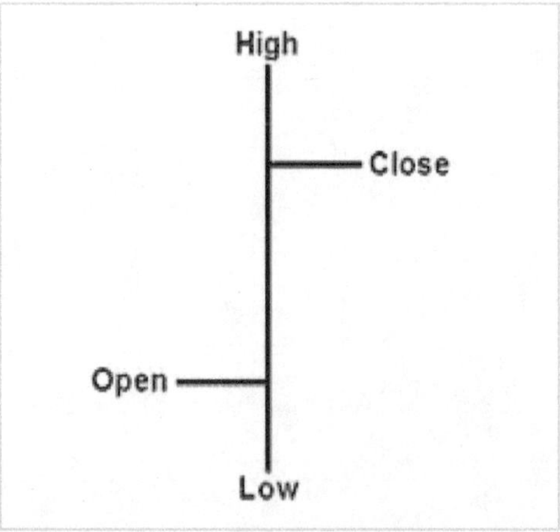

Seeing where a currency pair started the trading period compared to where it ended the trading period can help you to better identify trends. If the price closes higher than it opened, you know investors were bullish on the currency pair during the trading period. If the price closes lower than it opened, you know investors were bearish on the currency pair during the trading period. Here you can see an example of a bar chart.

Candlestick Charts

Candlestick charts provide the similar information as bar charts but in a slightly different format. Technical traders many times use candlestick charts instead of bar charts because it is easier to see and identify various trading patterns using candlestick charts. In fact, a complete line of technical analysis, Japanese candlestick-chart analysis was developed around these charts.

You create a candlestick chart by plotting a series of candlesticks across the chart. Each candlestick represents one trading period. To create a candlestick, you plot the high and low price of a trading period and connect them with a vertical line. This line is called the shadow of the candle. Next, you plot the opening price by drawing a horizontal line through the vertical line, or shadow. After you have plotted the opening price, you plot the closing price by drawing another horizontal line through the vertical line. Lastly, you fill in the area between the opening price and the closing price. This area is called the body of the candlestick.

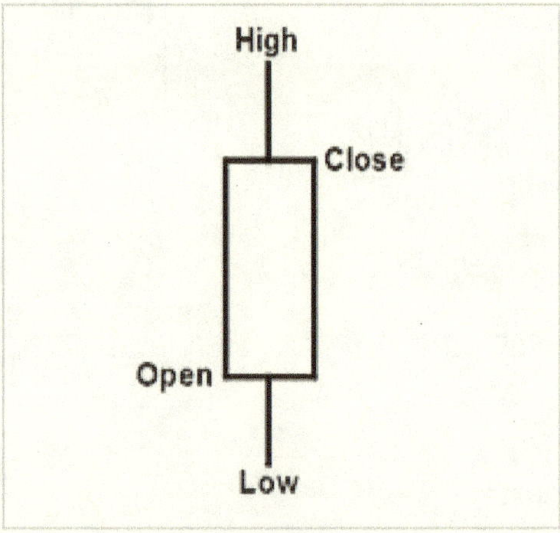

Knowing where a currency pair started the trading period compared to where it ended the trading period can help you to better identify trends. If the price closes higher than it opened, you know investors were bullish on the currency pair during the trading period. If the price closes lower than it opened, you know investors were bearish on the currency pair during the trading period.

You can see an example of a candlestick chart here.

CHAPTER 7:
Technical Indicators

Charts tell a market story. However, from time to time those charts may tell a story that you do not understand and you may need some help from an indicator. Technical indicators are the interpreters of the forex market. They look at price information and translate it into simple, easy to understand signals that can help you determine when to buy or when to sell a currency pair.

Technical indicators are based on mathematical equations that produce a value that is then plotted on your chart. For example, a moving average calculates the average price of a currency pair in the past and plots a point on your chart. As your currency chart moves forward, the moving average plots new points based on the updated price information it has. Ultimately, the moving average gives you a smooth indication of which direction the currency pair is moving.

Each technical indicator provides unique information. You will find that you will naturally gravitate toward specific technical indicators based on your trading style, but it is important to become familiar with several (not all) of the technical indicators that you have available.

You should also be aware of the weaknesses associated with technical indicators: Technical indicators look at historical price data, therefore, they are not guaranteed to know anything definite about the future. Technical indicators are divided into the following categories: Trending Indicators, Oscillating Indicators, Volume Indicators.

Trending Indicators

Trending indicators, as their name suggests, identify and follow the trend of a currency pair. Forex traders are most profitable when currency pairs are trending. It is therefore crucial for you to be able to identify when a currency pair is trending and when it is consolidating. If you can enter your trades shortly after a trend begins and exit shortly after the trend ends, you will be quite successful. Let us take a look at a few trending indicators.

Moving Average

Moving averages are the most basic trending indicator. They show you in what direction a currency pair is going and where potential levels of support and resistance may be. Moving averages themselves can serve as both support and resistance.

As we discuss moving averages, we will look at the following three topics: How are moving averages constructed, moving average trading signal, strengths of moving averages.

How Do You Build a Moving Average?

Moving averages are put together by finding the average closing price of a currency pair at any given time and then plotting these points on a chart. The result gives you a smooth line that follows the price movement of the currency pair.

You can manipulate the moving average by adjusting the timeframe that the indicator looks at to obtain the average price. Moving averages that look at fewer time periods to determine an average are usually more volatile. Moving averages that look at more time periods to determine an average are less volatile.

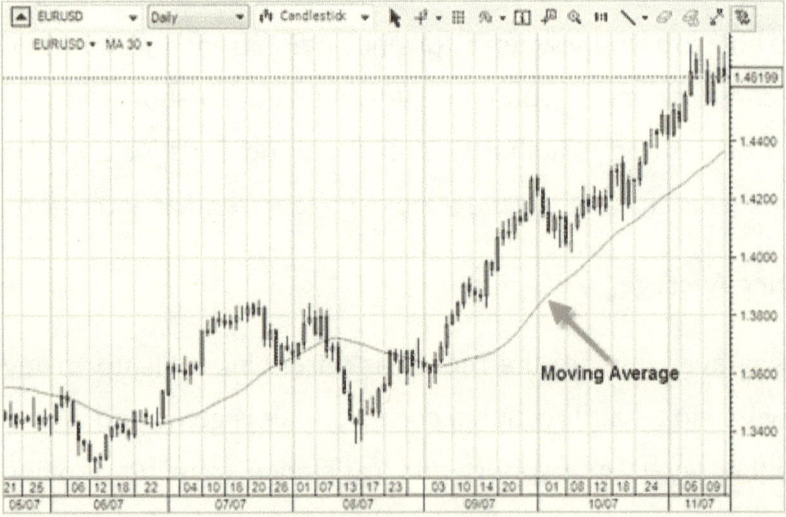

Moving Average Trading Signal

Moving averages provide useful entry and exit trading signals for currency pairs that are trending:

Entry signal - When a currency pair trending up bounces back up after hitting an uptrend moving average, or when a currency pair trending down pivots back down after hitting a downtrend moving average.

Exit signal - When you enter a trade on an up-trending currency pair, set a stop loss below the moving average. As the moving average rises, move your stop loss up along with the moving average. If the currency pair ever breaks far enough below the moving average, your stop loss will take you out of your trade.

When you enter a trade on a currency pair trending down, set a stop loss above the moving average. As the moving average falls, move your stop loss down along with the moving average. If the currency pair breaks far enough above the moving average, your stop loss will close your trade.

Strengths of a Moving Average

Moving averages enjoy the following strengths: They identify simple trends and are flexible enough to work in both short-term and long-term timeframes. In contrast to some indicators, they are very easy to understand.

CHAPTER 8:
Oscillating Indicators

Oscillating indicators are indicators that move back and forth as currency pairs rise and fall. Oscillating indicators can help you determine how strong the current trend of a currency pair is and when that trend is in danger of losing momentum and reversing. When the oscillating indicator moves too high, the currency pair is considered to be overbought (excessive buying and there are not enough buyers left in the market to push the currency pair higher). This indicates the currency pair is at risk of a reversal or a move lower.

When an oscillating indicator moves too low, the currency pair is considered to be oversold (excessive selling and there are not enough sellers left in the market to push the currency pair lower). This indicates the currency pair is at risk of losing momentum and begin a reversal to move higher. Let's take a look at the following oscillating indicator:

Moving Average Convergence Divergence (MACD)

The moving average convergence divergence (MACD) is an oscillating indicator that can show you when a trading momentum changes from bullish to bearish and from bearish to bullish. The MACD can also reveal to you when traders are becoming exhausted, which usually results in a trend reversal for the currency pair. The MACD is usually plotted below the price movements on a chart. To learn more about the MACD we will look at the following topics: Building the MACD, MACD trading signal, Strengths of the MACD.

Building the MACD

The moving average convergence divergence is built based on a series of moving averages and how they relate to one another. The standard MACD looks at the relationship between a currency pair 12-period and 26-period exponential moving average. Specifically, the MACD looks at the distance between these two moving averages. If the 12-period moving average is above the 26-period moving average, the MACD line will be positive. If the 12-period moving average is below the 26-period moving average, the MACD line will be negative.

The MACD line is accompanied by a trigger line. This line is a 9-period exponential moving average of the MACD line.

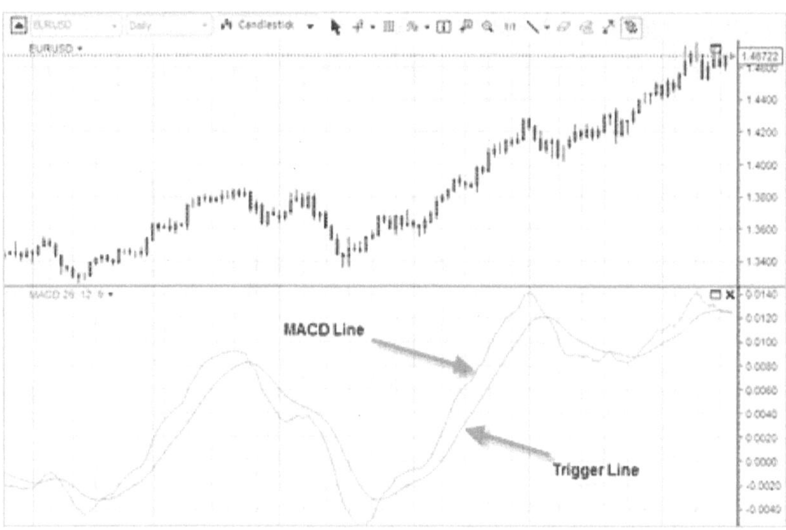

MACD Trading Signal

The moving average convergence divergence (MACD) gives trading signals as it crosses back and forth above and below the trigger line.

Entry signal - when the MACD crosses above the trigger line, you can buy the currency pair knowing that momentum has shifted from bearish to bullish. When the MACD crosses below the trigger line, you can sell the pair knowing that momentum has shifted from bullish to bearish.

Exit signal - when the MACD crosses back below the trigger line after you have bought the currency pair, you can sell the currency pair back knowing that momentum has shifted back to being bearish. When the MACD crosses back above the trigger line after you have sold the currency pair, you can buy the currency pair back knowing that momentum has shifted back to being bullish.

Strengths of the Moving Average Convergence Divergence (MACD)

The moving average convergence divergence (MACD) enjoys the following strengths: It helps you identify when the momentum of a currency pair changes and it helps you confirm the strength of current trends.

Volume Indicators

Currencies are traded on the inter-bank market and not on a central exchange, therefore, volume data for currency transactions is not available. Without volume data you cannot construct volume indicators. Therefore, we do not use volume indicators in forex trading. You can learn more about volume indicators as you diversify your trading into equities and futures.

CHAPTER 9:
Reversal Patterns

Forex traders often ask themselves the question, "how long will the trend continue?". Deciding whether a trend is over and if it is time to trade against the previous trend is difficult. You never know 100% if a currency pair is going to reverse and move in the opposite direction. Reversal patterns give you an early tip of when a currency pair is likely to turn around and begin a new trend and how far the currency pair is likely to move in the opposite direction. Let us review the following price reversal patterns:

Double Tops and Bottoms

Double tops and bottoms are reversal patterns that form as the price of a currency pair hits a support or resistance level twice before the pair pivots and moves in the opposite direction. Double tops are bearish reversal patterns and double bottoms are bullish reversal patterns. If a currency pair is in an uptrend, it will form a double top. If a currency pair is in a downtrend, it will form a double bottom. Double tops and bottoms usually form over longer periods of time. Double tops and bottoms have the following characteristics:

Resistance level (A) - horizontal level of resistance.

Support level (B) - horizontal level of support.

Breakout point (C) - the point at which the currency pair breaks up above the horizontal level of resistance (double bottom), or the point at which the currency pair breaks down below the horizontal level of support (double top).

Price projection (D) - the price to which the currency pair will most likely fall after it has broken out of the double-top formation, or the price to which the currency pair will most likely rise after it has broken out of the double-bottom formation.

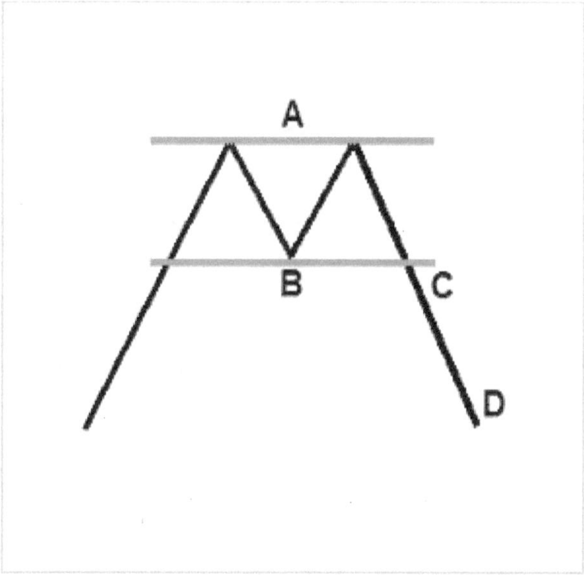

Head and Shoulders Tops/Bottoms

Head and shoulders tops are reversal patterns that form as the price of a currency pair hits a resistance level (forming the first shoulder), then breaks through the first resistance level and hits a higher resistance level (forming the head) and then hits the first resistance level again (forming the second shoulder).

Head and shoulders bottoms are reversal patterns that form as the price of a currency pair hits a support level (forming the first shoulder), then breaks through the first support level and hits a lower support level (forming the head) and then hits the first support level again (forming the second shoulder).

Head and shoulders tops are bearish reversal patterns and head and shoulders bottoms are bullish reversal patterns. If a currency pair is in an uptrend, it will form a head and shoulders top. If a currency pair is in a downtrend, it will form a head and shoulders bottom. Head and shoulders tops or bottoms usually form over long periods of time. Head and shoulders tops or bottoms all have the following five characteristics:

Left shoulder (A) - horizontal, level of resistance (head and shoulders top), or a horizontal, or slightly angled, level of support (head and shoulders bottom).

Head (B) - higher horizontal level of resistance (head and shoulders top), or a lower horizontal, or slightly angled, level of support (head and shoulders bottom).

Right shoulder (C) - horizontal, or slightly angled, level of resistance that is in line with the left shoulder (head and shoulders top), or a horizontal level of support that is in line with the left shoulder (head and shoulders bottom).

Neckline (D) - horizontal, or slightly angled, level of support (head-and-shoulders top), or a horizontal, or slightly angled, level of resistance (head-and-shoulders bottom).

Breakout point (E) - the point at which the currency pair breaks up above the neckline (head-and-shoulders bottom), or the point at which the currency pair breaks down below the neckline (head and shoulders top).

Price projection (F) - the price to which the currency pair will most likely fall after it has broken out of the head and shoulders top formation, or the price to which the currency pair will most likely rise after it has broken out of the head-and-shoulders bottom formation. The distance the currency pair is projected to move is equal to the distance between the head and the neckline.

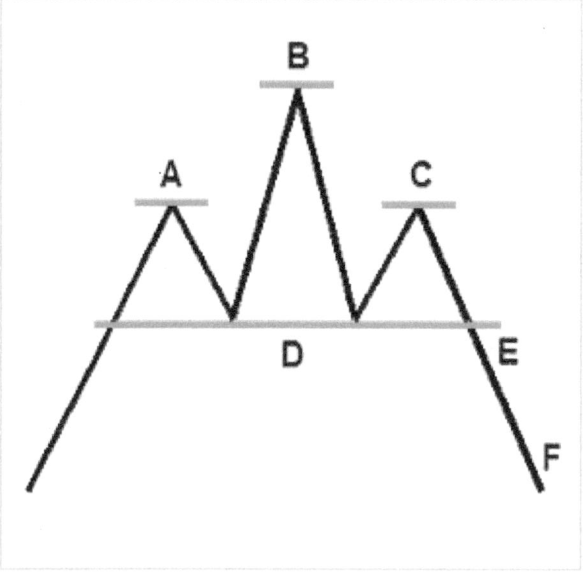

CHAPTER 10:
Using Multiple Time Frames

Traders of virtually every account size and risk tolerance trade the forex market. At any given moment, short-term scalpers and long-term fundamental analysis traders are looking at the same currency pairs and are trying to figure out how to place or adjust their trades. However, while they may be looking at the same currency pairs, they are not looking at the same chart timeframes. Short-term traders are most likely looking at 5-minute to 15-minute charts, while long-term traders are most likely looking at daily to monthly charts.

Trends, support and resistance lines, and technical indicators look much different on a 1-minute chart than they do on a daily chart. For example, you may look at a 1-minute chart of the EUR/USD and see that the pair appears to be in a downtrend. If you adjust your chart to a daily setting, you may see that the currency pair has been in an uptrend for weeks. So which chart is correct? Is the EUR/USD in an uptrend or a downtrend?....depends on your trading timeframe.

Forex traders trade with a bias toward the long-term trend. It has had a longer time to establish itself, and it will take a large breakout to change its direction. Obviously, if you see the fundamentals changing for a currency or a news announcement affecting a currency, you can trade against the long-term trend if you use good risk management. You should always be alert of trends and the support and resistance levels across multiple timeframes. This allows you to identify how strong various trends are. Using multiple timeframes on your charts helps you fine-tune your technical analysis.

You should analyze the following three charts in your technical analysis: Trend Chart (long term), Signal Chart, Timing Chart (short term). Once you have analyzed each timeframe, you can combine them to confirm a high-probability set up.

Trend Chart

The trend chart helps you identify the main trend that you should seek to trade with. If the currency pair in the trend chart is trending upward, you should be looking to buy the pair. If the currency pair in the trend chart is trending downward, you should be looking to sell it. To identify the timeframe that you should use for your trend chart, you first need to identify the timeframe you normally use on your trading (signal) charts. Once you have identified the timeframe of your signal chart, you should go up one timeframe to find the timeframe you should be using on your trend chart. The following is a list of common signal-chart time frames you can use to identify the appropriate time frame for your trend chart:

1-minute signal chart	=	15- to 30-minute trend chart
5-minute signal chart	=	1-hour trend chart
15- to 30-minute signal chart	=	4-hour trend chart
1-hour signal chart	=	1-day trend chart
1-day signal chart	=	1-week trend chart
1-week signal chart	=	1-month trend chart

For example, if you typically trade the EUR/USD looking at a 1-hour chart, you should use a 1-day chart for your trend chart. If you typically trade the EUR/USD looking at a 15-minute chart, you should use a 4-hour chart for your trend chart.

Once you have identified the timeframe you should use for your trend chart, all you need to do is determine what the prevailing trend on the chart is. You can use diagonal support and resistance levels or moving averages to identify the trend. You can see on our weekly EUR/USD that both the diagonal support level and the moving average indicate that this currency pair is in an uptrend.

If there is an uptrend on your trend chart, you should be looking for buy signals on your signal chart. If there is a downtrend on your trend chart, you should look out for sell signals on your signal chart. Once you have identified the trend, you now need to identify profitable trading signals.

Signal Chart

The signal chart is your most important chart. It provides the trading signals that tell you when to look for buying and selling opportunities based on the trading system you use. For example, if you typically use the commodity channel index (CCI) to help you identify trading signals, you will use the signal chart here. You will not use the indicator on the trend chart.

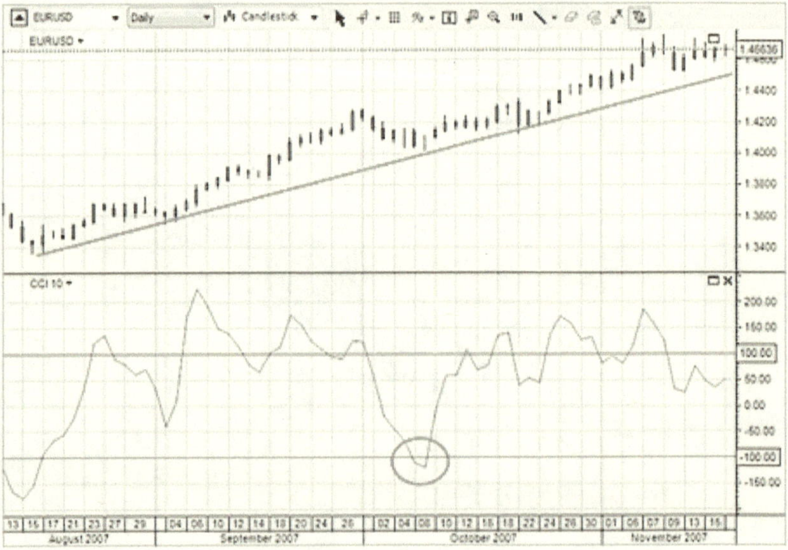

Using a signal chart together with a trend chart allows you to more accurately identify potential profitable trade signals. For example, if your trend chart shows the currency pair is in an uptrend, you should only look for buy signals on your signal chart. The best way to take advantage of a longer-term uptrend is to buy the currency pair. If your trend chart shows the currency pair is in a downtrend, you should only look for sell signals on your signal chart. The best way to take advantage of a longer-term down trend is to sell the currency pair.

The trend chart allows you to ignore the less profitable trading signals that you see on your signal chart. Since these trading signals are going against the longer-term trend, they are most likely to be unprofitable. Now that you have identified your trading signals, you need to determine exactly when to enter and exit your trades using your timing chart.

Timing Chart

The timing chart helps you time exactly when you should enter and exit a trade. Every pip counts when you are a forex trader so the more accurate you are with your entry and exit points, the more profits you earn for your account. The following is a list of common signal chart time frames you can use to identify the best timeframe for your timing chart:

1-minute signal chart	=	Tick timing chart
5-minute signal chart	=	1-minute timing chart
15- to 30-minute signal chart	=	5-minute timing chart
1-hour signal chart	=	15-minute timing chart
1-day signal chart	=	1-hour timing chart
1-week signal chart	=	1-day timing chart
1-month signal chart	=	1-week timing chart

You can use one of the following two methods when pinpointing your entry and exit signals on your timing charts:

1. Identify the trend and support and resistance levels
2. Use the same technical indicator you use to generate your trading signals

Identify the trend plus support and resistance if you see a buy signal on your signal chart, you want to see the currency pair in an uptrend on the timing chart. You also need to see that the pair price is closer to support than it is to resistance. This tells you it has room to move higher before hitting resistance. Of course, if it has just broken up through resistance, it could continue to move higher.

If you use a technical indicator like the commodity channel index (CCI), on your signal chart to generate buy and sell signals, you can also use that same indicator on your timing chart to help you identify when to enter or exit your trade. For example, if you did use the CCI on your signal chart and it gave you a buy signal, you would add the CCI to your timing chart and make sure it was giving you a buy signal on the timing chart as well. If the CCI is not giving a buy signal on the timing chart, you should wait until it gives a buy signal on the timing chart before you enter the trade.

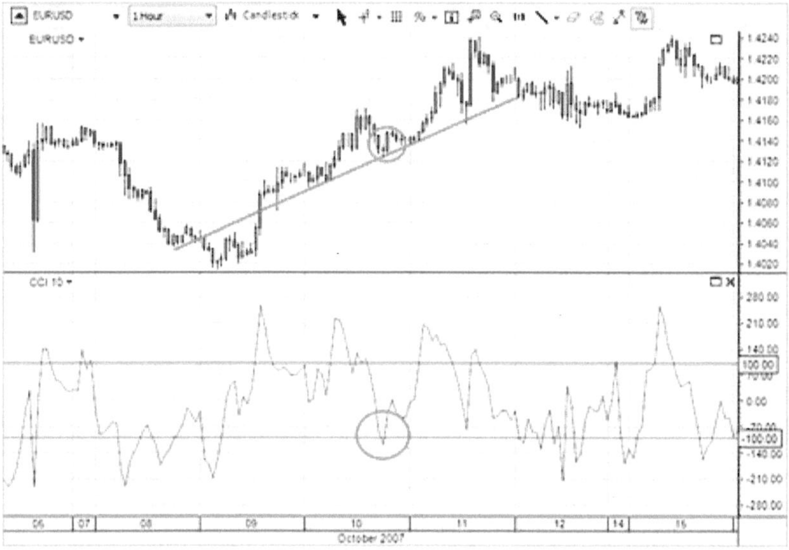
EURUSD
1 Hour
Candlestick
EURUSD
CCI 10
1.4240
1.4220
1.4200
1.4180
1.4160
1.4140
1.4120
1.4100
1.4080
1.4060
1.4040
1.4020
280.00
210.00
140.00
100.00
0.00
-100.00
-140.00
-210.00
-280.00
06
07
08
09
10
11
12
14
15
October 2007

CHAPTER 11:
High-Probability Trade Setup

Let us have a look at what a high-probability trade setup looks like using the multiple timeframe trading approach. We will analyze an example of the EUR/USD using a weekly chart as the trend chart, a daily chart as the signal chart and a 1-hour chart as the timing chart.

First, you check your trend chart to see what direction the currency is trending. As you can see on the EUR/USD weekly chart, the currency pair has been in an uptrend for a good amount of time. It would be unwise to fight this trend and attempt to sell the EUR/USD.

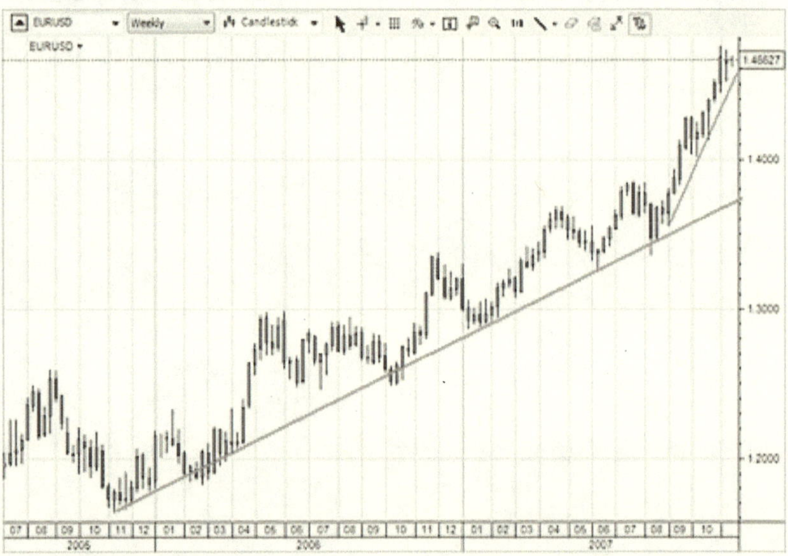

Next, you look at the signal chart to identify a good buy signal for the EUR/USD. In this example, we are looking at using the commodity channel index (CCI) to generate the trading signal. You can see on the daily EUR/USD chart that the CCI gave a buy signal on October 10th as it crossed from below -100 to above -100. The trend on the daily EUR/USD chart was also moving higher.

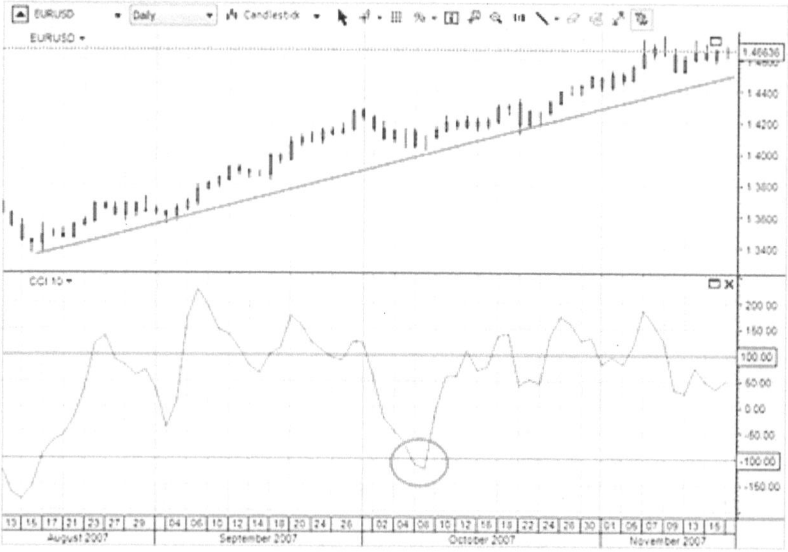

Finally, you look at the timing chart to identify an appropriate time to buy the EUR/USD. You can see on the 1-hour EUR/USD chart that the currency pair is in an uptrend at the time the trading signal was given on the signal chart. You can also see that the CCI on the 1-hour chart had just given a buy signal at approximately the same time the CCI on the signal chart had generated its signal.

Seeing the trading signal generated on the signal chart line up so well with the trend on the trend chart and the currency movement on the timing chart should give you increased confidence in the likelihood of your trade making money. Using multiple timeframes, as a rule, provides you with more accurate trading information.

CHAPTER 12:
Intermarket Relationships

The forex market is the most liquid financial market. While no other financial market can compete on the size of the forex market, the other markets do impact the forex market. For instance, the U.S. bond market can affect the value of the U.S. dollar (USD) just as the Canadian stock market can affect the value of the Canadian dollar (CAD).

To become a successful forex trader, you will need to understand the relationships that exist among the world's financial markets and how these relationships may affect the currency pairs you are trading. Oftentimes, you can receive an early warning of what is about to happen in the forex market by being alert of what is happening in other financial markets. For example, if you see the value of gold rising quickly, you can look for a similar rise in the value of the AUD/USD. Once you know what to be aware of you can take advantage of the similar correlations that the large institutional investors are watching. We will now focus on how the following markets affect the forex market: Commodity Market, Bond Market, Stock Market.

Commodity Market and the Forex Market

The global demand for commodities has linked the commodity market and the forex market closer. Virtually every economy around the world has to import some of its commodities. To buy these commodities, importers must exchange their currency for the currency of the economy from which they are importing the goods. This transaction drives the demand for the exporter's currency higher, which increases the value of that currency. This transaction also lowers the value of the importer's currency.

Three of the major currencies, the Canadian dollar (CAD), the Australian dollar (AUD) and the New Zealand dollar (NZD) are closely tied to commodity values because they are major commodity exporters. As the price of commodities rises, the value of these currencies normally rises. As the price of commodities falls, the value of these currencies typically falls. Each of these commodity currencies, as they are called, is affected differently by various commodities. For example, the Australian dollar is correlated with gold. As the price of gold climbs higher, the value of the Australian dollar also goes higher. As the price of gold goes lower, the value of the Australian dollar also falls. While this correlation isn't perfect, it is worth paying attention to.

Paying attention to events in the commodity market over the next years can lead you to profits in your forex trading. Be prepared to take advantage of not only the currencies that will strengthen as commodity prices increase but also of the currencies that will weaken.

Bond Market and the Forex Market

After the forex market, the global bond market is the second largest financial market in the world. Governments, institutions and individual investors all participate actively in the global bond market, and each one of these market participants is looking for the same thing, profits!

Government bonds make up the largest percentage of the global bond market. These bonds are typically viewed as risk-free investments because they are backed by the full good will and faith of national governments. However, not all government bonds are created equal. Some governments pay a higher interest rate for their bonds than others. International investors take these interest rates into account when they are deciding where to invest their money. Typically, bonds with higher interest rates are more attractive to investors as long as the economies backing the bonds are relatively stable.

Investors who wish to buy government bonds must buy these bonds with the currency of the represented government. If international investors wish to buy U.S. government bonds, they first exchange their currencies for U.S. dollars (USD). This increased demand for U.S. dollars (USD) drives the value of the USD higher. At the same time, the increased supply of international currencies on the market drives the value of these currencies lower.

Knowing which governments offer higher interest rates on their government bonds and which bonds are gaining popularity among international investors will help you know which currencies to buy and which currency to sell.

Stock Markets and the Forex Market

Individual investors globally seem to watch stock markets more closely than any other market. Stocks are exciting, they have been around for a while and most individual investors can relate to the companies in which they are buying stocks. When times are good in the stock market, money flows in. When times are bad in the stock market, money flows out.

Globalization has made it easier for investors from one country to invest in the stock markets of other countries. If investors see that stocks in the United States are performing well, they will rush to buy those stocks. If they see that stocks in Japan are starting to outperform stocks in Europe, they will take their money out of Europe and place it in Japan. Stocks are traded in the currency of the economy of which they are a part. To invest in stocks in the United States, foreign investors must first convert their currencies into U.S. dollars (USD). This increased demand for U.S. dollars drives the value of the USD higher. At the same time, the increased supply of international currencies on the market drives the value of these currencies lower.

Forex investors watch closely how the stock markets are performing. If the stock market in one country begins outperforming the stock market in another country, forex investors know that other investors are likely to move their money from the country with the weaker stock market to the country with the stronger market. This will drive the value of the currency for the country with the stronger stock market higher and the value of the currency for the country with the weaker market lower. By buying the currency from the country with the stronger market, then selling the currency from the country with the weaker market, you can potentially make a nice profit.

CHAPTER 13:
Fundamental Analysis Essentials

Economic Strength Boosts Currency Values

Strong economies generally have strong currencies, the two are linked. When an economy is performing well, it usually means that corporations are profitable, most of the workforce is employed and, in most cases, interest rates are increasing. These characteristics of a strong economy benefits you as a forex trader.

Rising interest rates are one of the most predictive indicator for rising currency values and central banks around the world determine interest rates in their respective economies. These central banks typically raise interest rates when inflation as measured by the consumer price index (CPI) and the producers' price index (PPI) starts growing too quickly.

Economic growth gives birth to inflation. The basics are, the stronger the economy is, the higher the demand for workers becomes. As the demand for workers goes up, wages for those workers also increases. The more money workers take home in their paychecks, the more money they have to spend at retail stores, on cars and on houses. As demand for goods and services increases, the price for those goods and services also increases, in other words, inflation.

Naturally, if central banks watch inflation indicators (like the CPI and PPI) in their decision-making process, you would assume they would also be interested in watching economic strength indicators to see how strong an economy is and they most certainly are. Central banks watch the following fundamental economic indicators to gauge the strength of an economy, and so should you:

Gross Domestic Product (GDP), Non-Farm Payrolls, Durable Goods Orders, Retail Sales.

Gross Domestic Product (GDP)

The Gross Domestic Product (GDP) is the broadest measure of aggregate economic activity available. Reported quarterly, GDP growth is broadly followed as the primary indicator of economic strength.

GDP represents the total value of a country's production during the period and consists of the purchases of domestically produced goods and services by individuals, businesses, foreigners and the government. Since GDP reports are often subject to noticeable quarter-to-quarter volatility and revisions, it is best to follow the indicator on a year-to-year basis. It can be valuable to follow the trend rate of growth in each of the major categories of GDP to determine the strengths and weaknesses in the economy. A high GDP figure is often associated with the expectations of higher interest rates, which is frequently positive, at least in the short term for the currency involved. This remains true unless expectations of increased inflation pressure is simultaneously undermining confidence in the currency.

Non-Farm Payrolls (USA)

This report is a measure of the number of people employed by non-farm businesses. Monthly changes in payroll employment reflect the net number of new jobs created or lost during the month and changes are widely followed as an important indicator of economic activity.

Payroll employment is one of the primary monthly indicators of aggregate economic activity because it encompasses every major sector of the economy. It is also useful to examine trends in job creation in several industry categories because the aggregate data can mask significant deviations in underlying industry trends. Large increases in payroll employment are seen as signs of strong economic activity that could eventually lead to higher interest rates that are supportive of the currency. If inflationary pressures are seen as building, this may undermine the longer term confidence in the currency.

Durable Goods Orders

Durable Goods Orders are a major indicator of manufacturing sector trends because the majority of industrial production is done to order. Often, the indicator excludes defense and transportation orders because these are generally much more volatile than the rest of the orders and can obscure the more important underlying trend.

Durable Goods Orders are also a measure of the new orders placed with domestic manufacturers for immediate and future delivery of factory hard goods. Monthly percent changes reflect the rate of change of such orders. Levels of, and changes in durable goods order are widely followed as an indicator of factory sector momentum. Rising Durable Goods Orders are normally associated with stronger economic activity and can therefore lead to higher short-term interest rates that are often supportive to a currency.

Retail Sales

Retail Sales are a measure of the total receipts of retail stores. Monthly percentage changes reflect the rate of change of such sales and are widely followed as an indicator of consumer spending. Retails Sales are a major indicator of consumer spending because they account for nearly one-half of total consumer spending and approximately one-third of aggregate economic activity.

Often, Retail Sales are followed minus auto sales because these are generally much more volatile than the rest of the Retail Sales and can therefore obscure the more important underlying trend.

Rising Retail Sales are often associated with a strong economy and therefore an expectation of higher short-term interest rates that are often positive for a currency in the short term.

Regional Economic indicators

Regional indicators like the Tankan reports are very important for JPY, and therefore have considerable impact on other markets in the region. Machine orders are also a critical piece of data since this affects exporting companies which in turn also affects the currency.

CPI figures from various countries especially Australia, Japan and China are usually a market mover and are closely watched by professional traders.

Purchasing Manager Index (PMI) numbers set the tone for the month and are an early indicator of economic activity in the region.

CHAPTER 14:
Trading Psychology

Forex traders have to not only compete with other traders in the forex market but also with themselves. Often as a forex trader, you will be your own worst enemy. As humans, we are often emotional. Our egos want to be validated, we want to prove to ourselves that we know what we are doing and that we are capable of taking care of ourselves. Our emotions and instincts can combine to provide us with trading successes every now and then. Most of the time, however, our emotions get the best of us and lead us to trading losses unless we learn to control them.

Many forex traders believe it would be ideal if you could completely separate yourself from your emotions. Unfortunately, that is very difficult, almost impossible, and some of your emotions may actually help improve your trading. The smart thing you can do is learn to understand yourself as a trader. Identify your strengths and your weaknesses, then select a trading style that is best for you. In this chapter, we will learn about the following four psychological biases that may be affecting your trading results and what you can do to overcome them: Overconfidence Bias, Anchoring Bias, Confirmation Bias, Loss Aversion Bias.

Overconfidence Bias

Overconfidence bias is an over-inflated belief in your skills as a forex trader. If you ever find yourself thinking that you have got everything figured out, there is nothing more to learn and money is yours for the taking in the market, you probably suffer from an overconfidence bias.

Dangers of Overconfidence

Overconfident traders tend to get themselves into trouble by trading too frequently (overtrading) or by placing extremely large trades as they go for the big win. In the end, an overconfident trader will end up either trading excessively, churning the trader's account or risking too much on the one trade that goes bad and wipes out most of their account balance.

Are You Overconfident?

If you want to know if you have any overconfidence tendencies, ask yourself if you have ever jumped right back into a trade you had just closed, not because you saw another entry opportunity, but because you could not believe that you were wrong? You can also consider if you have ever put more on a trade than you normally would just because you were sure the trade was going to be a winner? If you have, you need to be aware of those tendencies.

Overcoming Overconfidence

The best way to overcome an overconfidence bias is to establish a strict set of risk-management rules. These rules should at a minimum cover how many trades you will allow yourself to be in at one time, how much of your account you are willing to risk on any one trade and how much of your account are you willing to lose before you take a break from trading and evaluate your strategy. By limiting the number of trades you are willing to be in and the amount of risk you are willing to take, you can spread your risk out over your portfolio. Make failure survivable!

Anchoring Bias

Anchoring bias is a tendency to believe that the future is going to look or behave similar to the present. When you anchor yourself too closely to the present, you fail to see the dramatic changes that are possible as currency pairs fluctuate and the underlying fundamentals shift.

Dangers of Anchoring

Anchored traders usually get themselves into trouble by convincing themselves that the current trend will never end and a reversal in the economic strength of a particular country is next to impossible. Soon, they become emotionally attached to the previous trend of a currency pair and they continue to place trades that go against the new trend. With each trade they lose increasing amounts of money because they are bucking the trend.

Are You Anchoring?

If you want to know if you have any anchoring tendencies, question yourself, if you have ever lost money because you could not accept that the trend had ended. If you have, you need to be aware of that tendency.

Overcoming Anchoring

A good way to overcome anchoring is to look at multiple timeframes on your charts. If you usually trade on hourly charts, have a look at the daily and weekly charts occasionally to see where some of the longer-term levels of support and resistance are and what the long-term trends look like. You should also have a look at the shorter-term charts to see when the shorter-term trends are reversing. Expanding your perspective will help you avoid anchoring yourself to any one point.

Confirmation Bias

Confirmation bias is a propensity to look only for the information that confirms the beliefs that you already have. For instance, if you believe the EUR/USD is going to go up, you will seek the news, the technical indicators and the fundamental factors that support your belief.

Dangers of Seeking Confirmation

Traders who actively pursue confirmation of their beliefs tend to miss key warning signs that would have normally protected them from unnecessary losses. In an attempt to build a case for their beliefs, traders miss the facts. Ultimately, this leads to them fighting the trend and losing money with their trades.

Do You Seek Confirmation?

If you want to know if you have any confirmation bias tendencies, reflect on how often do you look for signs that you may be wrong in your analysis? If your answer is rarely or never, you may be a confirmation seeker, and you need to be aware of that.

Overcoming Confirmation Bias

One way to overcome confirmation bias is to find someone, or a network you can talk to about your trading. Hopefully the person or group that you talk with about your trading will not always agree with you. Speaking with traders who have diverse perspectives and ideas will help you look at your trades from different angles. Sometimes you will strengthen your convictions by talking with other traders. Other times, chatting with your trading partners will cause you to change course. Keeping an open mind will help you learn new strategies and avoid holding on too long to old beliefs.

Loss Aversion Bias

Loss aversion bias is based on the theory that the pain caused by losing $1,000 is greater than the joy that comes from gaining $1,000. To be more direct, fear is a more powerful motivator than greed.

Dangers of Loss Aversion

Traders who fear losses are much more likely to hold onto losing positions than traders who are able to accept short-term losses and move onto other more-profitable trades. Holding onto losing positions damages the stability of your account, not only by incurring losses, but it also keeps you out of better trades.

Do You Fear Losses?

If you want to know if you have any loss aversion weakness, ask yourself if you have ever held onto a losing trade past the point where you knew that you should have gotten out because you hoped the pair would turn around and erase the losses. If you have, you need to be aware of those tendencies.

Overcoming Loss Aversion

A good way to overcome a loss aversion bias is to trade with set stop-loss orders. Many traders tell themselves that they will trade with a mental stop-loss, a stop- loss that they think about and promise themselves they will execute if the currency pair ever reaches it. All too often, traders ignore this and fail to act on their mental stop-losses. They allow their emotions to dominate and they begin rationalizing their choice to stay in the trade until it turns around. As soon as you enter a trade, you must set your stop-loss order. Remove your emotions from the picture.

INTRODUCTION TO FUTURES

CHAPTER 15:
Futures Trading Strategies

Introduction

Welcome to *Futures Trading Strategies.* This section will ensure that you are equipped to begin using futures contracts as a trading instrument.

The section is primarily about futures trading, however the futures market can be, and often is, influenced by other markets. In the later chapters we will look at these markets individually and in the last chapter you will be introduced to exchange traded funds (ETFs), one of the most important and useful products created for individual investors in recent years.

CHAPTER 16:
Futures Overview

You have probably heard from friends or in the media of traders profiting from the futures market and you may have asked yourself if you could also profit from these global price fluctuations. The answer: yes, you too can participate in the futures market with a trading account.

The futures market is exciting and broad because it allows you to trade futures contracts on everything from cotton and sugar to interest rates and energies. You are not limited to just one sector of the global economy nor to strong economic periods. As a trader you can make money when prices are going up and also when prices are going down in the futures market.

Futures Contracts

The base of the futures market is the futures contract. To participate in the futures market you need to understand what a futures contract is and how it works. Let us begin with a basic definition and then we will move to a more in-depth understanding of the contracts and how you can profit from them. A futures contract is a contract between a buyer and a seller wherein the seller agrees to deliver a commodity/underlying instrument to the buyer on a specified date for a specified price.

Contracts

Buyers and sellers create futures contracts. This may seem odd at first if you are familiar with trading stocks which are issued by companies that determine the number of shares available. Futures contracts are different from stock market shares. While there is a finite number of stock market shares available, in contrast, there is an infinite number of potential futures contracts available. As long as there is a buyer and a seller, together they can create a futures contract.

Futures exchanges track how many contracts are created and list the amount as volume. Volume tells you how many contracts are created for each available commodity during each trading period. For example if you were looking at the natural gas futures contract and you saw a volume of 75,000 then you would know that 75,000 contracts had been created that day for the natural gas futures.

Volume can reveal a lot about what is going on with a futures contract and how many people are trading it, but it doesn't provide you the whole picture because not all volume comes from traders opening new trades. A sizable amount of volume is generated by traders who are already in trades and want to exit their trades.

Futures traders who are in a trade and want to get out of a trade have to create a new contract to offset their other contract.

As a futures trader you need to be aware of not only how many contracts have been created but also how many of those contracts remain active. High volume and high open interest are signs of good liquidity in the market, which means it should be very easy for you to quickly enter and exit your own trades at a small spread between the bid and ask price. Low volume and low open interest are signs of poor liquidity in the market, which means it will be most likely difficult for you to quickly enter and exit your trades at a good price.

Bid and Ask Price

Let us take a look at the buyers and sellers of the contracts. Futures contracts are quoted in two prices: a bid price and an ask price. The bid price is the price you receive when you sell your futures contracts. The ask price is the price offered when you want to buy futures contracts. The bid price is always lower than the ask price, and the difference between the two is called the spread. When a contract has low volume, the spread between the bid and the ask will be wide. When a futures contract has high volume, the spread between the bid and the ask will be thin or small. As a futures trader, or a trader in general, you want the spread to be as small as possible.

You can be either a buyer or a seller of a futures contract. The futures market provides great flexibility to buy or sell. As long as there is someone on the other side willing to sell a contract you want to buy, or to buy a contract you want to sell, you can create the contract.

Long and Short Positions

Two terms that you will hear often when discussing buying and selling futures contracts are long and short. To go long on a contract means to buy the contract. To go short on a contract means to sell the contract.

Typically, futures traders look to buy a contract when they believe the price is going to go up, and they want to sell a contract when they believe the price is going to go down. Your job as a futures trader is to determine in which direction you believe the price is going to move and trade accordingly.

Futures contract prices fluctuate daily and some futures exchanges limit the distance some contracts can move in one trading period. Futures contracts with maximum price fluctuation rules attached to them will stop trading if they move too far in one direction.

Futures contracts also have what are known as limit up and limit down thresholds. If the price of the futures contract moves up too high or down too low, trading on that contract will stop for a few minutes to allow the exchange to determine if trading should continue that day or if it should be halted to prevent panic on the exchange floor.

Hedgers and Speculators

Buyers and sellers of futures contracts are usually divided into two groups: hedgers and speculators.

Hedgers are traders who use futures contracts to hedge risks they face by dealing with the actual underlying commodities (ex. a wheat farmer) and the price swings associated with them.

Speculators are traders who use futures contracts to speculate on and hopefully profit from price changes in the underlying commodities. Speculators typically do NOT deal with the underlying commodities covered by the futures contract in their day-to-day business. You will most likely fall into this category of futures traders.

Speculators buy futures contracts on commodities that they believe are going to increase in value and sell futures contracts on commodities that they believe are going to fall in value. Speculators play an important role in the futures market. They provide liquidity for hedgers who are looking to offset their risk. Speculators take on risk when they enter a trade. In plain terms, hedgers pass their risks on to speculators who hope to profit from them.

Now that you have a basic understanding of who the buyers and sellers in the futures market are, let us take a look at the commodities those buyers and sellers are trading.

CHAPTER 17:
Commodity Futures

When many people think of the commodity futures market they think about trading coffee or orange juice. While these commodities trade on the futures exchanges, they make up a smaller portion of the trading activity. Nowadays oil contracts, natural gas contracts, interest-rate contracts, grains and others dominate the futures market.

The futures market offers a broad and diverse array of contracts which you can trade. You can profit from falling oil prices and you can take advantage of a raising currency. You can divide the available futures contracts into two categories: commodity futures and financial futures.

Commodity futures are futures contracts that are based on a physical commodity that you can raise, grow, mine and transport from place to place. Commodity futures comprise the following sectors:

- Agriculture
- Base Metals
- Energies
- Meats
- Precious Metals
- Softs

Financial futures are futures contracts that are based on financial products like bonds and stock indices. Financial futures comprise the following futures sectors:

- Bonds
- Currencies
- Short-term Interest Rates
- Stock Indices

Within each of these sectors you will find contracts ranging from sugar and soya beans to silver and copper, and each contract has a unique personality. We will cover several of these sectors and the contracts within them in later chapters.

CHAPTER 18:
Contracts Dates, Exchanges and Margins

Every futures contract has a specified date on which it expires and a specified price at which the seller must provide the commodity and the buyer must pay for it. We will take a look at the dates involved with a contract, and then we will take a look at the actual delivery of the underlying commodity.

Futures contracts have three key dates of which you need to be familiar with: Notice date, Expiry date, Delivery date.

The **Notice date** is the first day the seller of a futures contract can give the buyer of the contract notice to expect delivery of the underlying commodity. For example, if you sell a crude copper futures contract, you can give notice to the buyer of the contract that you will be delivering the actual copper. In reality you will not do this, you will instead offset your contracts before taking delivery.

The **Expiry date** is the day that the futures contract expires. It is also the last trading day for the contract. Futures contracts expire every month, however, not every commodity is traded each month, but there are always some commodity contracts available each month. You need to check the specific commodity you are trading to see when the contract expires.

Every futures contract has a unique ticker symbol that tells you what the underlying commodity is and when the contract expires. Each ticker symbol is broken up into three parts: the instrument identification, the month of expiration and the year of expiration. For example the ticker symbol for a Crude Oil contract that expires in July of 2017 is CLN17. CL represents the instrument, N represents the month of expiration, 17 represents the year of expiration.

The monthly commodity symbols are below:

F	January
G	February
H	March
J	April
K	May
M	June
N	July
Q	August
U	September
V	October
X	November
Z	December

The **Delivery date** is the last date by which the underlying commodity must be delivered from the seller to the buyer. The delivery date is also known as the settlement date. However, the seller does not have to wait until the delivery date to deliver the commodity. The seller can deliver at any time during the delivery period, the period between the first notice date and the delivery date.

Again, there is no need to worry about delivering or receiving delivery of a commodity you are trading. You should offset your positions before your contracts expire. In fact most traders, both speculators and hedgers, offset their positions. Only a small percentage of futures contracts actually go to delivery.

It is important to know that there are two types of delivery on futures contracts: physical delivery and cash-settled delivery. Physical delivery occurs when the buyer receives the underlying commodity from the contract. Cash-settled delivery occurs when, instead of trying to receive an intangible asset like the S&P 500, the buyer receives the cash equivalent of what the underlying asset would be worth.

You now have the basic information that you need to understand what a futures contract is. Let us take a look at where and how you actually trade a futures contract.

Futures Brokerages

A futures broker or a bank are your portal to the futures market. Your futures broker provides you with access to a trading platform and an account that allows you to buy and sell contracts. Your broker also provides you with the tools that you will need to research and monitor your trades.

Futures Exchanges

When you place a trade to buy or sell a contract your bank or broker sends that trade to a futures exchange for execution. In the past your trade would have been sent to the trading pit on the floor of the exchange for whatever contract you were trading. Floor traders would negotiate prices and your trade would be filled. Some trades are still executed on physical trading floors, many more are now executed online electronically. Complex software match buyers with sellers and execute trades in fractions of a second. Technological advances like these have made trading more efficient.

Here is a list of some of the exchanges on which you can trade:

Chicago Board of Trade (CBOT), via ECBOT
Chicago Mercantile Exchange (CME), via GLOBEX
New York Mercantile Exchange (NYMEX), via GLOBEX
New York Board of Trade (NYBOT), via ICE NYBOT
GLOBEX
Eurex
Euronext
ICE
Borsa Italiana
London International Financial Futures Exchange (LIFFE)
Spanish Official Exchange (MEFF)
OMX Stockholm (SSE)

Now that you know where you can trade futures contracts, let us take a look at how you actually go about placing your trades.

Margin Requirements

For many, one of the most tricky concepts to understand as a new futures trader is the concept of margin. When you trade a futures contract you do not pay for the full value of the underlying commodity up front as you would when trading stocks. Instead, you place a trade and deposit your margin with your futures broker verifying that you have sufficient money to cover any losses you may have from the trade.

For example, to buy a 1,000 barrels crude oil futures contract, instead of having to pay $50,000 for 1,000 barrels of crude oil (at a market rate of $50 per barrel) up front you would only need $3,500(for example purposes only) in your account as margin. This allows you to be able to withstand some losses on this trade should they come.

The margin you set aside when you enter a trade is called your initial margin. After executing a trade you may not need to maintain the same level of margin. When you are in a trade, you only need to meet what is called your maintenance margin requirement, which, depending on the exchange, is typically lower. Maintenance margin is the amount of money you must set aside to remain in a trade. In our crude oil example your maintenance margin requirement would only be $3,000, compared to the initial margin requirement of $3,500.

Margin requirements are set by the futures clearing houses. Margin requirements are also not permanently fixed. The exchange/clearing houses can adjust minimum margin requirements at any time. Your broker can raise their margin requirements if they want to. Your broker can also issue what is known as a margin call if your margin levels fall below acceptable minimums based on losses you have accumulated on your trades or increases in margin requirements. If you receive a margin call then you must deposit more money into your account to cover your margin obligations.

Once you have met your margin requirement, you can enter your trade. You can buy or sell a futures contract using either a market or a limit order. A market order is a buy or sell order that instructs your broker to place the trade at the current market rate. A limit order is a buy or sell order that instructs your broker to place the trade at a specific price or better.

If you want to enter or exit a trade quickly and ensure you get in or out then you should use a market order. If you are okay with waiting to enter or exit a trade until the price is just right then you could use a limit order to ensure you get the price you desire.

CHAPTER 19:
Commodity Suppliers

Futures contract prices rise and fall with the seasons of the year. The movements appear to flow in what seems to be a predictable rhythm, prices seem to always go up at certain times of the year and down at other times of the year. Whether it is spring planting season for agricultural commodities, a summer vacation low for equities, or December demand for precious metals, there always seems to be something on the calendar that influences supply and demand in the market.

This ebb and flow of prices is certainly not an exact science, many factors other than seasonality will have an influence on the price of a futures contract too, but knowing how the futures contracts you are watching progress through the seasonal calendar can help you plan your trading year and prepare for future trades.

To help give you a broad overview of your trading calendar and which futures contracts you may want to be buying or selling at any given time, we will discuss the characteristics of the four seasons of the year: Winter, Spring, Summer, Autumn.

Suppliers

Before we move into the seasons, it is important to know who the major suppliers of each commodity are so you can better understand why the change of seasons affects each one.

In today's global economy, the commodities we consume can come from virtually anywhere in the world. Often we hear about economic mega-centers like the United States, the European Union and China and we begin to think that everything we buy comes from these places. When you are dealing with raw commodities, however, that is not always true. Countries like Brazil, Argentina, India and even Peru are dominant producers of many of the commodities that trade on the global futures markets.

As you think about commodity producers, especially those that produce agricultural commodities it is important to remember which hemisphere they are in because that will have an influence on crop cycles. When it is summer in the Northern Hemisphere, it is winter in the Southern Hemisphere, and vice versa.

Northern Hemisphere: Is the half of earth that is north of the equator which is around 90% of the earth's total human population.

Southern Hemisphere: Is the half of earth that is south of the equator which is around 10% of the earth's total human population.

Let us review the top three producers for each of the following commodities: Energies, Precious Metals, Agriculture.

Energy

Crude Oil - The top three global producers of crude oil are as follows:

1. Russia
2. Saudi Arabia
3. United States

Natural Gas - The top three global producers of natural gas are as follows:

1. Russia
2. United States
3. Iran

Precious metals

Gold - The top three global producers of gold are as follows:

1. China
2. Australia
3. Russia

Silver - The top three global producers of silver are as follows:

1. Mexico
2. China
3. Peru

Agriculture

Soybeans - The top three global producers of soybeans are as follows:

1. United States
2. Brazil
3. Argentina

Wheat - The top three global producers of wheat are as follows:

1. China
2. India
3. Russia

Corn - The top three global producers of corn are as follows:

1. United States
2. China
3. Brazil

Sugar - The top three global producers of sugar are as follows:

1. Brazil
2. India
3. China

Coffee - The top three global producers of coffee are as follows:

1. Brazil
2. Vietnam
3. Colombia

Cotton - The top three global producers of cotton are as follows:

1. China
2. India
3. United States

CHAPTER 20:
Seasonality and the Futures Market

Now that you know who the major producers of each commodity are, let us take a look at what you should be watching for in each season of the year.

January, February & March

Sugar

Winter in the Northern Hemisphere is harvest time for sugarcane and sugar beets. The sugarcane and sugar beet harvest has a noticeable impact on supply in the market. If it is a good harvest, supply will increase, which should decrease the price of sugar. If it is a poor or weak harvest, supply will decrease, which normally should increase the price of sugar.

April, May & June

Crude Oil

Crude oil prices typically begin to increase in the spring as gasoline producers begin to anticipate the well-known summer driving season in the United States.

Corn

Spring in the Northern Hemisphere is *planting* time for corn. The corn planting season has a direct impact on supply in the market. If it is a strong planting season, supply will increase, which should result in a decrease the price of corn. If it is a poor planting season, supply will decrease, which should increase the price of corn.

Spring in the Southern Hemisphere is *harvest* time for corn. The corn harvest has a direct impact on supply in the market. If it is a good harvest, supply will increase, which should decrease the price of corn. If it is a poor harvest, supply will decrease, which should increase the price of corn.

Cotton

Spring in the Northern Hemisphere is planting time for cotton. The cotton planting season has a direct impact on supply in the market. If it is a strong planting season, supply will increase, which should decrease the price of cotton. If it is a poor planting season, supply will decrease, which should increase the price of cotton.

Soybeans

Spring in the Northern Hemisphere is *planting* time for soybeans. The soybean planting season has a direct impact on supply in the market. If it is a productive planting season, supply will increase, which should decrease the price of soybeans. If it is a poor planting season, supply will decrease, which should increase the price of soybeans.

Spring in the Southern Hemisphere is *harvest* time for soybeans. The soybean harvest has a direct impact on supply in the market. If it is a good harvest, supply will increase, which should decrease the price of soybeans. If it is a poor harvest, supply will decrease, which should increase the price of soybeans.

Sugar

Spring in the Northern Hemisphere is *planting* time for sugarcane and sugar beets. The sugarcane and sugar beet planting season has a direct impact on supply in the market. If it is a productive planting season, supply will increase, which should decrease the price of sugar. If it is a poor planting season, supply will decrease, which should increase the price of sugar.

Autumn in the Southern Hemisphere is *harvest* time for sugarcane and sugar beets. The sugarcane and sugar beet harvest has a direct impact on supply in the market. If it is a good harvest, supply will increase, which should decrease the price of sugar. If it is a poor harvest, supply will decrease, which should increase the price of sugar.

July, August & September

Crude Oil

Crude oil prices typically jump the most during the summer season as the amount of drivers on the road increase during the summer and producers of winter heating oil are increasing their supplies to sell at the start of the autumn.

Wheat

Summer in the Northern Hemisphere is traditional harvest time for wheat. The wheat harvest has a direct impact on supply in the market. If it is a good harvest, supply will increase, which should decrease the price of wheat. If it is a weak harvest, supply will decrease, which should normally increase the price of wheat.

Coffee

Winter in the Southern Hemisphere is harvest time for coffee. The coffee harvest has a clear impact on supply in the market. If it is a strong harvest, supply will increase, which should decrease the price of coffee. If it is a bad harvest, supply will decrease, which should increase the price of coffee.

Sugar

Winter in the Southern Hemisphere is also harvest time for sugarcane and sugar beets. The sugarcane and sugar beet harvest has a direct impact on supply in the market. If it is a strong harvest, supply will increase, which should decrease the price of sugar. If it is a poor harvest, supply will decrease, which should increase the price of sugar.

October, November & December

Crude Oil

Crude oil prices typically decrease the most during the autumn months as people begin to drive less. Also, people tend to buy most of their heating oil at the beginning of the season leaving less demand during the rest of the season.

Wheat

Autumn in the Northern Hemisphere is planting time for wheat. The wheat planting season has a direct impact on supply in the market. If it is a productive planting season, supply will increase, which should decrease the price of wheat. If it is a bad planting season, supply will decrease, which should increase the price of wheat.

Corn

Autumn in the Northern Hemisphere is harvest time for corn. The corn harvest has a direct impact on supply in the market. If it is a good harvest, supply will increase, which should decrease the price of corn. If it is a poor harvest, supply will decrease, which should increase the price of corn.

Cotton

Autumn in the Northern Hemisphere is harvest time for cotton. The cotton harvest has a direct impact on supply in the market. If it is a good harvest, supply will increase, which should decrease the price of cotton. If it is a weak harvest, supply will decrease, which should increase the price of cotton.

Soybeans

Autumn in the Northern Hemisphere is harvest time for soybeans. The soybean harvest has a direct impact on supply in the market. If it is a good harvest, supply will increase, which should lower the price of soybeans. If it is a poor harvest, supply will fall, which should increase the price of soybeans.

Sugar

Autumn in the Northern Hemisphere is also *harvest* time for sugarcane and sugar beets. The sugarcane and sugar beet harvest has a direct impact on supply in the market. If it is a good harvest, supply will increase, which should lower the price of sugar. If it is a poor harvest, supply will fall, which should increase the price of sugar.

Spring in the Southern Hemisphere is *planting* time for sugarcane and sugar beets. The sugarcane and sugar beet planting season has a direct impact on supply in the market. If it is a productive planting season, supply will increase, which should decrease the price of sugar. If it is a poor planting season, supply will decrease, which should increase the price of sugar.

Coffee

Spring in the Southern Hemisphere is blooming time for coffee. The coffee blooming season has a direct impact on supply in the market. If it is a good blooming season, supply will increase, which should decrease the price of coffee. If it is a bad blooming season, supply will decrease, which should increase the price of coffee.

CHAPTER 21:
Intermarket Analysis

The futures market is the most diverse global financial market. While no other financial market can compare to the diversity of the futures market, other financial markets do have an impact on the futures market. For instance the U.S. bond market can influence the value of the U.S. Dollar Index futures contract just as the Japanese yen can affect the value of the Nikkei 225 Index futures contract.

To become a successful futures trader you will need to recognize the relationships that exist among the world's financial markets and comprehend how these relationships may affect the futures contracts you are trading.

Sometimes you can receive an early warning of what is going to happen in the futures market by watching what is currently happening in other financial markets. For example if you see the value of the AUD/USD currency pair rising quickly, you can look for a corresponding rise in the value of the gold futures contract. Once you know what to look out for, you can take advantage of the same correlations that the large institutional investors are watching. In this section we will be focusing on how the following markets affect the futures market: forex, bond, stock.

The Forex Market and the Futures Market

The rise of global demand for commodities has tied the futures market and the forex market closer together. Virtually every country around the world has to import some of the commodities it consumes. To buy these commodities importers typically must exchange their currency for the currency of the country from which they are importing their goods. This transaction drives the demand for the exporter's currency higher, with a corresponding increase in the value of that currency. This transaction also drives the supply of the importer's currency higher and therefore the value of that currency decreases.

Three of the major currencies - the Canadian dollar (CAD), the Australian dollar (AUD) and the New Zealand dollar (NZD) are closely related to and influenced by commodity values because they are major commodity exporters. As the price of commodities rises the value of these currencies typically rises. As the price of commodities falls the value of these currencies typically falls.

Each of these commodity currencies, as they are known amongst forex traders, is correlated with a different commodity. For example gold futures are highly correlated with the Australian dollar. As the price of the Australian dollar rises the value of gold futures typically also increase. As the price of the Australian dollar dips the value of gold futures also falls. While this correlation is not perfect it is worth paying attention to.

Futures traders can also buy and sell futures contracts that directly represent the currencies themselves. You can buy the futures contract for the Canadian dollar if you think this currency is going to increase in value. Or, you can sell the futures contract for the Japanese yen if you believe this currency is going to decrease in value. Paying attention to what is happening in the forex market during the trading sessions could therefore lead you to greater profits in your futures trading.

The Bond Market and the Futures Market

The global bond market is the second largest financial market in the world. Governments, institutions and individual investors all participate actively in the global bond market. Each one of these market participants is looking for the same thing, a profitable return on investment.

Government bonds make up the largest percentage of the global bond market. These bonds are typically viewed as risk-free investments because they are backed by the full goodwill and faith of national governments. However not all government bonds are created equal or achieve equality. Some governments pay a higher interest rate for their bonds than others. International investors take these interest rates into consideration when they are deciding where to invest their money. Typically bonds with higher interest rates are more attractive to investors, as long as the economies backing the bonds are relatively stable.

Investors who desire to buy government bonds must buy these bonds with the currency of the represented government. If international investors wish to buy U.S. government bonds then they must first exchange their currencies for U.S. dollars. This increased demand for U.S. dollars drives up the value of the U.S. Dollar Index futures contract. At the same time the increased supply of some international currencies on the market drives down the value of the futures contracts for those currencies.

Knowing which governments offer higher interest rates on their government bonds, and likewise which bonds are gaining popularity among international investors, will help you to identify which currency futures contracts to buy and which currency futures contracts to sell. Fortunately for traders the international bond market rarely changes directions instantaneously. Instead it cycles in longer-term and somewhat predictable trends that you can exploit.

You can also trade futures contracts on the government bonds themselves. If you see that demand for Japanese or Swiss bonds is increasing, for instance, you can buy the futures contract for either of these bonds

Stock Markets and the Futures Market

Individual investors around the world seem to watch stocks more closely than any other market. Stocks are exciting, they have been around for a while and most individual investors can relate to the companies in which they are buying stock. When stocks are performing well, money from around the globe flows in to buy the hot stocks. When stocks are performing poorly, money flows out as international investors sell their shares.

Futures investors can take advantage of the general increases and decreases in stock markets around the world by investing or trading in the futures contract representing the indices from the major global stock markets. For instance, to take advantage of a rising stock market in France, a futures investor can buy the futures contract for the CAC 40. Likewise, to take advantage of a falling market in the United Kingdom, a futures investor can sell the futures contract for the FTSE 100.

Globalization has also made it easier for investors from one country to invest in the stock markets of other countries. If investors see that stocks in the United Kingdom are performing well, they will look to buy those stocks. If they see that stocks in Japan are starting to outperform stocks in Europe, they may redirect their money out of the U.K. and put it into Japan in the hope of earning higher rates of return on their investments.

Stocks are priced in the local currency. To invest in stocks in the United Kingdom foreign investors must first convert their currencies into British Pounds. This increased demand for British Pounds drives up the value of British Pound futures contracts. As this occurs the increased supply of international currencies on the market, a supply that is disproportionate to demand, drives the value of the futures contracts for these currencies lower.

Futures investors watch closely how the stock markets in major countries are performing. If the stock market in one country begins outperforming the stock market in another country then futures investors know that other investors are likely to consider moving their money from the country with the weaker stock market to the country with the stronger stock market. This will drive up the value of the futures contract representing the currency of the country with the stronger stock market. And, meanwhile, the value of the futures contract representing the currency of the country with the weaker stock market will be down. By buying the futures contract for the currency from the country with the stronger stock market, and by selling the futures contract for the currency from the country with the weaker stock market, you can potentially make a handsome profit.

CHAPTER 22:
Spread Strategies

Futures traders are not limited to simply buying and selling one futures contract at a time to take advantage of price movements in the market. They have the ability to buy and sell offsetting contracts in what is known as a spread trade.

Spreads take on various forms but they all have two things in common:

1. They provide a hedge against adverse price movement
2. They are designed to take advantage of the changes in price relationships between two futures contracts.

Spreads provide a hedge against adverse price movement because you simultaneously buy and sell futures contracts when you enter a hedge. As the value of one contract goes up the value of the other contract goes down. For instance if you incur losses on the futures contract you bought as part of the spread, you can partially offset them with the gains you will realize on the contract you sold as part of the spread. Conversely if you incur losses on the futures contract you sold as part of the spread, you can partially offset them with the gains you will realize on the contract you bought as part of the spread.

Spreads take advantage of changes in price relationships. Imagine, for instance, that you see crude oil futures contracts trading on one exchange for $99 per barrel and crude oil futures trading on another exchange for $100 per barrel. You could enter a spread trade by buying the crude oil futures contract that was trading at $99 per barrel and selling the crude oil futures contract that was trading at $100 per barrel. If the two prices eventually converge, you will make a profit.

In this section we will be focusing on the following three types of spread trades: Inter-delivery spreads, Inter-commodity spreads, Inter-exchange spreads

Inter-Delivery Spreads

An inter-delivery spread is one in which a trader buys a futures contract with a certain delivery month and simultaneously sells the same futures contract with a different delivery month on the same exchange. Here's the simple breakdown:

Futures Contract:	Same
Delivery (Expiration) Month:	Different
Exchange:	Same

Inter-delivery spreads are also sometimes referred to as intra-market spreads or calendar spreads.

For example if you want to buy the July Chicago wheat contract (traded on the Chicago Board of Trade, or CBOT) because you believe prices are going to go up in the short term, but you want to hedge some of your exposure to the downside. You can accomplish this by buying the July wheat contract and simultaneously selling the September wheat contract. If the price of wheat increases in the short term, the price of the July wheat contract will probably increase faster than the price of the September wheat contract causing you to make more money on the July contract than you will lose on the September contract. However, if the price of wheat decreases in the short term, the price of the July wheat contract will also probably decrease faster than the price of the September wheat contract, causing you to lose some money on the July contract but enabling you to offset some of your losses with your gains on the September contract.

Traders divide inter-delivery spreads into two categories: bull spreads and bear spreads. A bull spread is an inter-delivery spread where you buy the nearby contract (the contract that will expire the soonest) and sell the deferred contract (the contract that will expire the latest). Traders utilize bull spreads when they believe prices are going to increase in the near-term.

The example above of buying the July wheat contract and selling September's equivalent is a good example of a bull spread.

A bear spread is an inter-delivery spread where you sell the nearby contract and buy the later month contract. Traders utilize bear spreads when they believe prices are going to decrease in the near-term.

For example, if you want to sell the July wheat contract because you believe prices are going to go down in the short term but you want to hedge some of your exposure to the upside. You can accomplish this by selling the July wheat contract and simultaneously buying the September wheat contract. If the price of wheat decreases in the short term then the price of the July wheat contract will probably decrease faster than the price of the September wheat contract causing you to make more money on the July contract than you will lose on the September contract. On the other hand if the price of wheat increases in the short term then the price of the July wheat contract will also probably increase faster than the price of the September wheat contract, causing you to lose some money on the July contract but allowing you to offset some of those losses by your gains on the September contract.

Inter-Commodity Spreads

An inter-commodity spread is a spread in which a trader buys a futures contract with a certain delivery month and simultaneously sells a different, but related, futures contract with the same delivery month on the same exchange. Here is the execution example:

Futures Contract:	Different
Delivery (Expiration) Month:	Same
Exchange:	Same

Imagine again that you want to buy the July Chicago wheat contract because you believe prices are going to go up in the short term, but you want to hedge some of your exposure to the downside. However you don't currently see any price advantage in using an inter-delivery spread. Instead you decide to use an inter-commodity spread and hedge the risk you face (as a consequence of buying a July wheat contract) by selling a July Chicago corn contract.

Wheat and corn are two different commodities but they are related. They both have relatively similar growing seasons, both are grain, and both are important in the global food supply. Now, however, you believe the price of wheat is going to increase faster than the price of corn. To take advantage of this price discrepancy you decide to buy the July wheat contract and sell the July corn contract. If the price of wheat increases faster in the short term than the price of corn, the price of the July wheat contract will probably increase faster than the price of the July corn contract allowing you to make more money on the July wheat contract than you will lose on the July corn contract. On the other hand if the price of wheat decreases faster in the short term than the price of corn, the price of the

July wheat contract will also probably decrease faster than the price of the July corn contract causing you to lose some money on the July wheat contract but enabling you to offset some of your losses with your gains on the July corn contract.

Inter-Exchange Spreads

An inter-market spread is a spread in which a trader buys a futures contract with a set delivery month and simultaneously sells the same futures contract with the same delivery month on a different exchange. Here is the breakdown:

Futures Contract:	Same
Delivery (Expiration) Month:	Same
Exchange:	Different

Inter-exchange spreads are also sometimes referred to as inter-market spreads. Imagine that you want to buy the July Chicago wheat contract because you believe prices are going to rise in the short term, but that you also want to hedge some of your exposure to the downside. However, instead of hedging by using an inter-delivery spread or an inter-commodity spread, you decide to use an inter-exchange spread by hedging your long July Chicago wheat contract with a short July Kansas City wheat contract (traded on the Kansas City Board of Trade).

Chicago wheat and Kansas City wheat are quite similar. If one contract is trading at a higher price than another contract, you can buy the contract that is trading at the lower price and sell the contract that is trading at the higher price. By doing so you are buying low and selling high. If the two prices eventually converge once more then you will make a profit.

CHAPTER 23:
Diversification

Diversification is the practice of spreading your funds across a broad range of unrelated investments. Just like a football coach strategically places his players across the field to take advantages of changes in the game and exploit weaknesses of the opponent, you should be looking to strategically place your money across the futures market to be prepared to profit from whatever sector of the market that may begin to move.

Diversification can help protect your trading portfolio from sudden and deep losses. Let us say if you were to take all of your money and buy futures contracts on crude oil only to see the price of oil turn around and plummet in a single day. It would not take too big of a move to wipe out your entire account. Now imagine if you were to take some of your money and buy a few futures contracts on crude oil, a few futures contracts on corn, a few futures contracts on the S&P 500 and a few futures contracts on gold. Even if the price of oil dropped dramatically causing you to lose money on that trade you would still have three other trades that had not been affected by the change in the price of oil.

Obviously, you should not invest in random futures contracts just to diversify your account. You must always believe the trade you are making has the potential to be a profitable trade. But you should look to spread your risk across multiple attractive trades.

Diversification comes in different forms and sizes. In this section, we will take a look at two ways to profitably diversify your account: Commodity Diversification, Strategy Diversification.

Commodity Diversification

Perhaps the most obvious and straightforward form of diversification is diversifying amongst various commodities. As mentioned, chances are low that you will lose money on a crude oil contract, a corn contract, an S&P 500 contract and a gold contract at the same time. These futures contracts are not all affected by the same market forces. Conversely, some futures contracts are closely related. And if you only invest in closely related futures contracts, you could lose money on each contract. For instance, crude oil and natural gas are closely related, corn and wheat are closely related, the S&P 500 and the FTSE 100 are closely related and gold and silver are closely related.

Traders who achieve optimal commodity diversification look to spread their trades out among the various futures sectors. To review, the following sectors comprise the commodity futures category:

- Agriculture
- Base Metals
- Energies

- Meats
- Precious Metals
- Softs

The following sectors comprise the financial Futures category:

- Bonds
- Currencies
- Short-term Interest Rates
- Stock Indices

To put it in perspective, you have many futures sectors to choose from when you are a futures trader. You do not need to limit yourself to just one or two of those sectors. You can trade a contract in the softs sector, the bonds sector, the energies sector and the agriculture sector and diversify your risk.

Naturally, you should conduct a thorough analysis before placing any trade. Remember, you should not diversify among random contracts just for diversity's sake. You should always have a reason to buy or sell a specific contract.

If you are just getting started in your futures trading, it may take a while before you feel comfortable trading contracts from all the futures sectors, and that is just fine. There is no pressure to trade everything and specializing is often best in the beginning.

Strategy Diversification

Diversification relates not only to *which* futures contracts you choose to buy and sell but also to *how* you decide to buy or sell those contracts. Strategy diversification can be just as important to your overall success as a futures trader as commodity diversification.

You have learned many different trading strategies throughout this book. You have learned about trading with price patterns, trading with technical indicators, and trading various spread strategies. Now it's time to begin using these various strategies.

For example, if you are looking across the different market sectors because you want to maintain a healthy amount of commodity diversification, and you notice that the futures contracts in one of the sectors (ex. precious metals) are moving sideways while the futures contracts in one of the other market sectors (ex. energies) are moving higher in a strong up trend. Certainly, you could diversify your account and buy some contracts in the precious metals sectors and some contracts in the energies sector and achieve a high level of commodity diversification, but is that really the most effective way to deploy your money into these trades?

Buying the contracts in the energies sector is probably a good idea because those contracts are currently in up trends. However, buying the contracts in the precious metals sectors seems like a waste of time because those contracts are channeling sideways. Perhaps a more effective use of your money would be to implement a spread strategy, like an inter-delivery spread, that takes advantage of futures contracts that are moving sideways. By doing so, you would not only ensure that you achieve your desired level of commodity diversification but also ensure that you are using the appropriate trading strategy for what the market provides you. Try taking aspects of this approach with your futures trading. If you find one strategy is not working, try another one. You are only limited by your imagination and your willingness to be creative.

In the end, if you can diversify your trading across multiple futures contracts and implement a few different trading strategies to take advantage of whatever circumstances the market is throwing at you, you will find you are well on your way to becoming a successful futures trader.

INTRODUCTION TO CRYPTOCURRENCIES

CHAPTER 24:
Exchange Traded Funds

Exchange traded funds (ETFs) are investment funds that are traded on stock exchanges. While they are not mutual funds, they do offer all of the benefits of diversification that you would enjoy when trading a mutual fund. ETFs also enjoy all of the benefits of liquidity that you have from trading individual shares. In plain terms ETFs are funds that trade like a stock.

ETFs offer instant diversification because, when you buy an ETF, you buy a piece of a fund that incorporates multiple assets. ETFs are like a large asset pool into which fund managers place various assets such as shares, bonds and commodities. When you buy an ETF you buy wholesale ownership of the pool and its contents as a whole, not piecemeal ownership of the individual contents.

You can make money with an ETF. As the value of the assets within the pool increases so does the overall value of the pool. Conversely, as the value of the assets within the pool decreases so does the overall value of the pool. In other words as the assets within an ETF increase in value the value of the ETF increases, and as the assets within an ETF decrease in value the value of the ETF decreases.

Instant Diversification

ETFs give you the ability to simultaneously own multiple assets without having to buy each asset individually. Imagine, for instance, the trading costs that would accumulate and the capital you would need to have in your account if you had to buy each share within the S&P 500 individually.

Diversification can also help protect you from unsystematic risk. For instance if you own only one of the shares in the Nikkei 225 Index, and that share loses value, you will lose money on your investment. However if you own the entire Nikkei 225 Index via an ETF, and that same share goes down, you have 224 other shares around it that are likely to ensure the value of the entire index either remains stable or climbs higher.

Many of the most popular ETFs track broad market indices. The following are just a few examples:

S&P 500

Dow Jones Industrial Average

FTSE 100

DAX Index

Nikkei 225

FTSE/Xinhua China 25 Index

NASDAQ 100

CAC 40 Index

Many ETFs also track various market sectors such as the following:

Information technology
Energy
Materials
Industrials
Telecommunication
Utilities
Health care
Financials

Open Market Trading

ETFs are freely traded on stock exchanges just like regular shares. As long as the stock exchanges on which the ETFs trade are open you can buy or sell any ETF. This is an advantage over mutual funds.

Mutual funds typically are only traded at the end of the market day once all of the assets within the funds can be valued. At that point the funds are assigned a closing value for the day, and you can buy or sell the funds at the closing value. Unfortunately during trading days when the assets within the funds are losing value you must hold onto the funds until the end of the day regardless of how much value the funds are losing. To conclude, whether you see the value of an ETF increasing or decreasing during the trading day you can buy or sell the ETF to take advantage of the price movement.

You can protect your ETF trades by setting stop loss orders. Because ETFs are freely traded you can set stop-loss orders that may take you out of your trades during the market day when your pre-determined price is hit. If you were trading mutual funds to obtain diversification, you would not have this ability because you can only buy or sell mutual funds at the end of the trading day after the markets have closed. So it wouldn't matter if your trigger price was hit during the market day because you would not be able to exit your trade.

Stop Loss Orders

Stop loss orders allow you to implement appropriate risk management measures in your account. Consequently, you can simultaneously protect your investment capital by both diversification and stop-loss orders.

Lower Fees

When you give your money to a manager to invest you usually have to pay that manager a fee. Typically the more active a role the manager plays in the investment decisions the larger the fee you will have to pay. ETFs usually have lower fees because they are passively managed, unlike many funds, including mutual funds that are actively managed.

Many ETFs track a specific index, market sector and so on. Since the composition of most stock indexes and share sectors barely changes, the managers of most ETFs do not often need to change the holdings within the fund. Consequently, because these managers do not play as active a role they charge a lower fee.

Most mutual fund managers, on the other hand, make daily decisions regarding what assets they are going to add to their portfolios, what assets they are going to keep in their portfolios and what assets they are going to remove from their portfolios. This active management and the trading fees it produces boost the fees that mutual fund managers charge their clients.

CHAPTER 25:
The Guide to Mastering Bitcoin & Cryptocurrencies

Introduction

We begin our journey away from the world of government issued currencies to cryptocurrencies. The first chapters will give you a solid introduction to the cryptocurrency universe, where you will be introduced to a wide range of topics from blockchain to mining. You will also be exposed to the mechanics behind one of the most popular cryptocurrencies. The emphasis shifts in the remaining chapters to practical applications for trading.

Note: Throughout this section the words digital, crypto and cryptocurrency will be used interchangeably.

CHAPTER 26:
What is Bitcoin (BTC)?

Bitcoin is a decentralized digital currency (a digital asset). It's not a stock, a tangible asset, or an actual coin. No government owns it. You can transfer money quickly without governments or banks for a low fee. In its base form it is a big spread sheet, a secure public ledger. Before money, there were ledgers. This is how primitive societies kept track of who had and did what. Cryptocurrencies, as many say, are a natural evolution in the history of money, from bartering, to coins, to paper money, to digital.

Secure?

How secure is it? What if someone or some group hacked the ledger? Even if 40-49% were hacked, the majority would have the correct info (the ledger is decentralized). As long as the majority of the ledgers agree, the transaction is valid. If some entity tried for a 51% (majority) attack, you should be aware that an attack of this magnitude would require funds in the area of 500 million dollars to carry out. In addition, an attack of this size would be noticed relatively quickly by the network.

Keys and Wallets

There is a secret private key and a public verification key. The private key is what gives you access to your account. The public key is used to send or receive money, unless you have the private key you are unable to move a coin. Your "wallet" contains your private key. A Bitcoin wallet is loosely the equivalent of a physical wallet. Your wallet also shows your transactions on the ledger.

Why Bitcoin (BTC)?

Moving money or settling transactions is expensive and cumbersome. There are the obstacles of currency spreads, taxes, banking fees, and transaction days. The average foreign wire transfer fee in the United States and elsewhere is expensive. From corporate treasurers to the migrants who want to send money home to relatives, all dislike the traditional transfer fees. With Bitcoin, money can be moved for a nominal fee. This has the ability to assist billions of persons who do not have access to banking services. This is also an option to those suffering under high Inflation and currency controls in countries (at the time of writing) like Venezuela, Zimbabwe, etc.

A Basic BTC Transaction

A) Sarah wants to send Phillip 20 Bitcoins
B) Sarah has 100 Bitcoins
C) Sarah prepares a "transaction" and sends it out onto the blockchain*
D) Enough "miners" confirm that the transactions in a block* are legitimate. Phillip decides how much validation he needs. Even if a few miners are not trustworthy, the bulk of them will be and we can trust that the transaction between them is valid.
E) Bitcoins are transferred

*Blockchain: A **public** record/ledger of Bitcoin transactions

*Block: Is a record in the blockchain that contains and confirms waiting transactions

BTC Believers

The list of people with a positive view of Bitcoin includes influential names such as Bill Gates, Richard Branson, and Peter Thiel. Other backers include venture capitalists (VC's) and Bitcoin startups with over 1 Billion US dollars invested so far. Another example is BitAngels, a Bitcoin focused investor group looking to scale startups.

Some of the major companies considering or already accepting Bitcoin payments are, Subway, Wordpress, Virgin Galactic, Reddit, Wikipedia, Shopify, OKCupid, Amazon, Paypal, and Ebay. This is only a snapshot. For small business owners, this creates a new pool of potential clients.

Bitcoin History (Quick Version)

Satoshi Nakamoto: What We Know

- Author of the white paper and original Bitcoin software
- Not a real name. The real identity is unknown, could be; she, he, or they/corporate entity
- Rarely heard from since 2010
- Owns many Bitcoins from early mining

History

2009-2011: Enthusiast in forums spreading ideas but no real traction. Genesis block established January 3, 2009

2012-13: First bit of attention from investors, risk takers, entrepreneurs

2013-2014: Big VC's began investing

2015: Wall Street and institutions began seriously investing

2016-present: Retail traders, "man on the street" enter in noticeable numbers

Bitcoin's Many "deaths"

Bitcoin has "died" 150+ times. Below are just a few of the wildly inaccurate predications of Bitcoin's demise.

- August 11, 2013 "Why Bitcoin Is Doomed To Fail" – moneygeek | $93.43
- November 16, 2013 "Bitcoin Is A Joke" – Business Insider | $433.57
- May 4, 2017_ "The Beginning of the End for Bitcoin" – Daily Reckoning | $1541.90
- July 12, 2017 "Bitcoin acceptance is virtually zero and shrinking" – Yahoo Finance | $2410.55

Bitcoin Crashes and Troubles

- 2011-2013: Saw major price bubbles and crashes

- February 2014: Mt. Gox, a Bitcoin exchange, filed in Tokyo for bankruptcy. The company lost almost 750,000 of its customers' Bitcoins, plus 100,000 of its own, worth around $473 million at the time of filing. Mt. Gox believes that the bitcoins were stolen, and blamed hackers.

Suggestion: Do due diligence, *but* be careful about using the results of one private company as judgment on an entire industry.

Bitcoin Anonymous?

Bitcoin is **not** a 100% anonymous, the addresses are public keys. The addresses however are not connected to your real world identity. To create a new identity you simply create a new public key, this is called pseudonymity.

Blockchain based currencies are publicly and permanently traceable, every coin has a history and you can see all previous transactions. True anonymity requires pseudonymity and unlinkability. In other words, different transactions of the same user with the network should not be linkable to each other. Without anonymity, privacy is much worse than traditional banking!

Unlinkability

With unlinkability it is hard to link the different addresses of the same user. It is also difficult to connect different transactions of the same user and to link the sender of a payment to its recipient. Why is this needed? Many Bitcoin services require a real identity. For example, online wallets and exchanges, some regulated, keep records which removes your anonymity with these services.

CHAPTER 27:
The Mechanics of Bitcoin

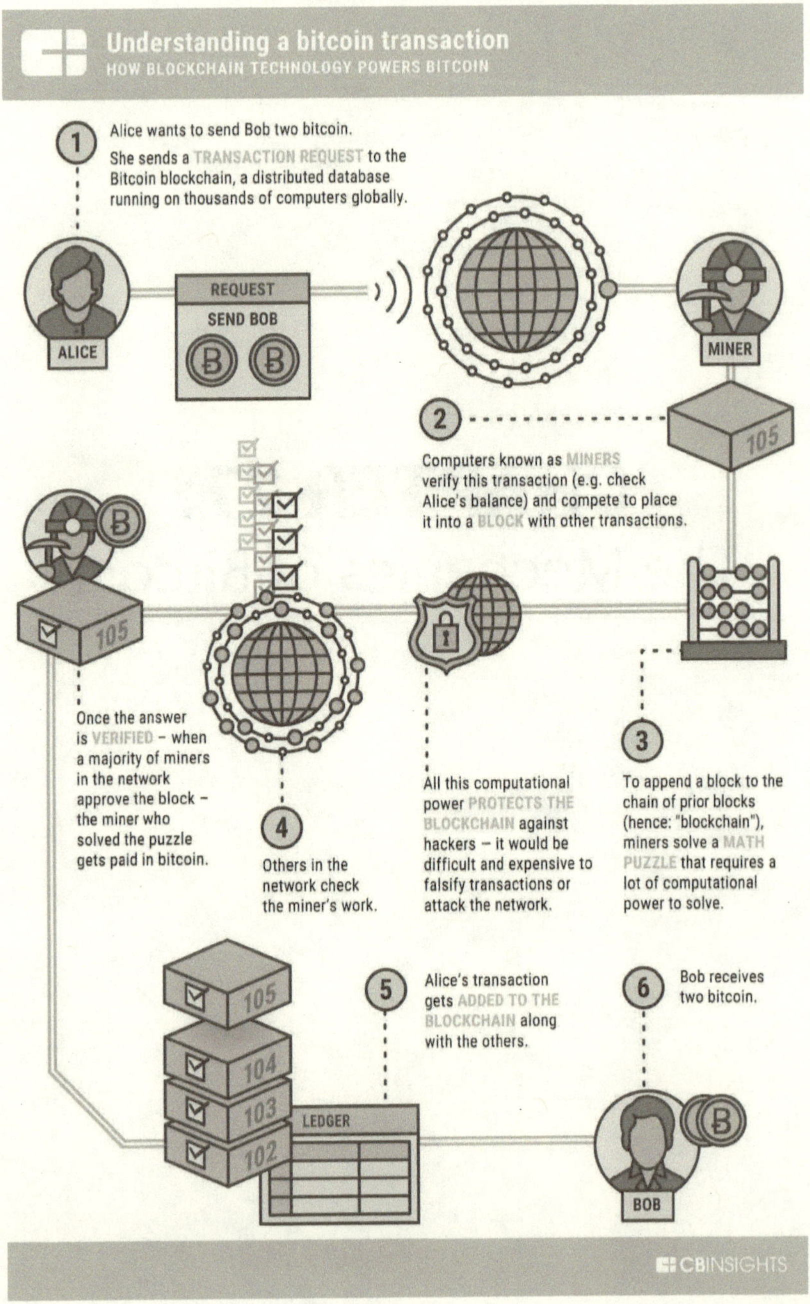
Understanding a bitcoin transaction
HOW BLOCKCHAIN TECHNOLOGY POWERS BITCOIN
1
Alice wants to send Bob two bitcoin.
She sends a TRANSACTION REQUEST to the Bitcoin blockchain, a distributed database running on thousands of computers globally.
ALICE
REQUEST
SEND BOB
MINER
2
Computers known as MINERS verify this transaction (e.g. check Alice's balance) and compete to place it into a BLOCK with other transactions.
105
3
To append a block to the chain of prior blocks (hence: "blockchain"), miners solve a MATH PUZZLE that requires a lot of computational power to solve.
All this computational power PROTECTS THE BLOCKCHAIN against hackers – it would be difficult and expensive to falsify transactions or attack the network.
4
Others in the network check the miner's work.
Once the answer is VERIFIED – when a majority of miners in the network approve the block – the miner who solved the puzzle gets paid in bitcoin.
105
104
103
102
LEDGER
5
Alice's transaction gets ADDED TO THE BLOCKCHAIN along with the others.
6
Bob receives two bitcoin.
BOB
CBINSIGHTS

Bitcoin Core Software: The Rulebook of Bitcoin

The Bitcoin Core Software is open source, (MIT license). Open source is software with "source code" that anyone can inspect, modify, and enhance. This "source code" is the code that programmers can manipulate to change how a piece of software or program works.

Storage of Bitcoins

We will take a look at some of the ways that you can store and keep track of coins. There are hot (online) and cold (offline) storage options available for your coins.

Software Wallets – Benefits/Risks

A software wallet is a relatively simple method. You store your key in a file on your computer or phone. It is convenient, but if the device is lost, the key is lost which means your coins are lost. In other words, it is only as secure as your device. If your device is hacked and the key is leaked then most likely your coins will be stolen.

Online Wallets – Benefits/Risks

An online wallet is similar to a local software wallet but it's in cyberspace. A site stores the keys and you log in to access the wallet. It is convenient with nothing to install and it works on multiple devices. The security concerns are well-known. It is vulnerable if the site is compromised (internally or externally).

Be aware that your private key(s) are stored on another server, with thousands of other keys which could entice hackers to launch an attack.

Paper & Hardware Wallets – Benefits/Risks

A paper wallet is printing your public and private keys on paper and locking up the paper. More secure than the online counterparts, however, a paper wallet can be torn, water-damaged, stolen, or destroyed in many other ways. It is important to make multiple copies and keep them secure.

Hardware wallets are USB shaped stand-alone devices that generate keys while making a transaction. They do need to be plugged into your computer while making the transaction. The wallets are secured from potential computer malware because they generate private keys offline, on the devices themselves. They are convenient and relatively easy to use. They provide backup options, plus they can also be secured with a password to combat theft. Overall, hardware wallets are the more secure option.

Bitcoin Exchanges

Exchanges accept deposits of Bitcoins (BTC) and fiat currencies ($, €) with a promise to pay back on demand. They allow customers to make/receive Bitcoin payments, buy/sell Bitcoins for fiat currencies, and match Bitcoin buyers with sellers.

An example of a common transaction: My account at the exchange has $5000 + 3 BTC, I use the exchange to buy 2 BTC for $1000 each, end result: my account has $3000 + 5 BTC.

Regulations: Banks vs Exchanges

With traditional banks, the government typically:

- Imposes minimum reserve requirements
- Insures deposits

With exchanges, the regulations varies substantially from country to country. However, there are several that have earned the trust of the market.

Bitcoin Geek Details

- 100 M *Satoshis* per Bitcoin
- 21M total Bitcoins
- 1 MB(megabyte*) each block, which is about 7 transactions per second, keep in mind
- VISA can process 2,000-10,000 transactions per second
- *One megabyte is one million bytes of information

CHAPTER 28:
Bitcoin Mining

The mining process is one of the keys to preventing fraud. Miners confirm the authenticity of the Bitcoin transactions contained in a block. They do this by taking each transaction's corresponding data and using it to complete a math problem. The solution is known as a "hash", a shorter unique string of digits that has the important transaction information within the block. The miners are rewarded in return with 12.5 coins for their efforts.

Miners

Bitcoin miners join the network, listen for transactions and validate all proposed transactions. They also listen for new blocks, maintain the blockchain and when a new block is proposed, they validate it. The total supply of Bitcoins is 21 million. Unless the rules change they run out in 2040.

Mining Requirements and Hardware

Mining needs massive amounts of electricity! This is used to perform the computations 24/7, 365 days a year. Next on the list, are the high cooling requirements, this is needed to protect the machines. The ideal temperature in mining centers is between 15-25°C (59-77°F).

Hardware

On a high-end PC it would take years to find a block, therefore you need something a lot faster. Bitcoin ASICs are Bitcoin mining hardware. They outperform other platforms for Bitcoin mining in speed and efficiency. Bitcoin ASIC chips generally can *only be used for Bitcoin mining*. With ASIC chips the time needed to find a block drops significantly. They are designed to be run constantly for life and they also require significant expertise.

Mining Pools

Solo mining is very difficult. Even with the latest mining hardware, unless you have access to incredibly cheap power, you could eventually end up spending all your money on electricity bills. Therefore, small miners pool their risk and the pool's participants attempt to mine blocks. They distribute the revenues (transaction fees, along with newly created Bitcoins) to members based on how much work they have performed, minus the pool manager's fee.

The first pools appeared in 2010 and by 2015 around 90% of mining was pool-based. However, today major mining centers dominate. Professional mining centers are possible when the following conditions are in place: cheap power, good network and a cool climate. Since they operate 24/7, 365 days a year, a larger mining center (20,000+ machines), uses 40 megawatts of electricity per hour, the average amount used by 12,000 homes during the same period. They can pay up to $40,000 a day for electricity, even with the discounts that they normally receive.

Mining Block Rewards

Currently, block rewards are the majority of miners revenue. It is expected that in the future transaction fees will dominate. The Bitcoin block mining reward halves every 210,000 blocks, and the current coin reward will decrease from 12.5 to 6.25 coins.

CHAPTER 29:
Bitcoin Community and Politics

A Bitcoin Improvement Proposal (BIP) is a formal proposal for changes to Bitcoin. It includes technical specifications and the basis for them. Anyone in the world can propose a BIP. It is up to the Bitcoin community of users, miners, developers, and investors to vote and decide whether or not to implement proposals.

In the Bitcoin community, the Core Developers rule changes are followed by default. What if users don't like a rule change? They can exit or exercise their right to "fork" the rules or software. A fork is a change to the software of a digital currency that creates two separate versions of the blockchain with a shared history.

Soft & Hard Fork Possibilities

Soft forks can lead to new signature schemes and extra per block metadata. Hard forks can lead to changes to size limits and changes to the mining rate.

A hard fork is a permanent divergence in the blockchain, it occurs when non-upgraded nodes can't validate blocks created by upgraded nodes that follow newer consensus rules. A node is a computer that connects to the Bitcoin network.

After a hard fork, if the fork was meant to start an altcoin (alternative currency), the altcoin goes its separate way, they coexist. If the fork reflected a fight over the future of Bitcoin then the sides fight for market share to be seen as the "real Bitcoin" one wins, the other might fade away. In the case of Bitcoin Cash they co-exist.

Hard fork example: Bitcoin Cash is similar to Bitcoin, except that it increases the size of a block from 1MB to 8MB. Why was this needed? If a transaction doesn't make it onto a block that is sent into the network for validation, it has to wait, and this slows down the process. Increasing the size of a block results in faster transactions.

Who Has The Power In Bitcoin?

There are many opinions on who has the "real" power in Bitcoin. For now we will work with the principle that it depends on who wins the fight if they fail to agree. Below is a brief description of the different players.

Bitcoin Power Brokers

Investors - Determine whether Bitcoin has any market value
Bitcoin Core Developers - They write the rulebook
Miners - Write the history and validate transactions
Merchants and their customers - They generate the primary demand and long-term price for Bitcoins

In addition to the above players, there is the Bitcoin Foundation (founded 2012). The foundation pays Core Developers and speak to governments as the representative of Bitcoin.

CHAPTER 30:
Regulations

Governments are very much aware of Bitcoin. The attention is attracted because you have untraceable digital cash that circumvents capital controls and countries can't stop Bitcoin value from flowing in or out.

So can no one stop Bitcoin? Hmm...Bitcoin could be banned through regulation of the communication operators (communication is subject to regulation). Bitcoin is a type of internet traffic that can be stopped as any other. If a government were to decide suddenly that no one in their country can access Bitcoin, they could mandate that telecoms ban access by blacklisting exchanges and others in their infrastructure. China, in 2017 cracked down on exchanges but not much happened, Bitcoin price only went higher in the weeks following. Recently, I read of one company currently working on a global satellite network that will broadcast blockchain data down to every corner of the planet so that people can use Bitcoin without needing the internet.

The First Wave of Regulations

The New York State BitLicense was a part of the first wave of regulations to hit the crypto Market. If your business involves New York or a New York State Resident, anyone engaging in any of the following is required to obtain a license:

- Virtual currency transmission
- Storing, holding, or maintaining custody or control of virtual currency on behalf of others

- Buying and selling virtual currency as a customer business
- Performing exchange services as a customer business
- Controlling, administering, or issuing a virtual currency

Undesirable Negatives

Untraceable digital currency, unfortunately does have a list of undesirable negatives. It can make certain crimes easier to do, for example, kidnapping, extortion, tax evasion and the sale of illegal items. One example of this was the scandalous Silk Road website. It operated from February 2011 to October 2013. It was the largest online market for illegal drugs. Payments were made in Bitcoins, and the site held the coins for security while the goods were shipped.

Ross Ulbricht was the brain behind Silk Road. He went by several aliases, the best known were "Frosty" and "Dread Pirate Roberts." He tried to cover his trail, but the authorities were able to connect the dots. He was arrested in October 2013 and is now serving time in jail with a life sentence. The government seized 174,000 Bitcoins and they were later auctioned to the public.

The two lessons to be learned are, first, it's difficult to remain anonymous for a long time. The other, is that it's hard to move from the underground to the legitimate economy without attracting attention from law enforcement.

CHAPTER 31:
Bitcoin and Altcoins Trading

Cryptos provide volatility, as traders we love this, it is sweet music for us. Why? If you place a trade and nothing happens then you have just paid the spread to your broker for nothing. Trading is a business (or you should treat it as one), for you to recover your cost of the transaction (the spread) you need and want volatility.

Rumors and panics add to the volatility. There can also be extreme sensitivity to news, 20% daily moves are **not** uncommon. The autumn of 2017, even by crypto standards, the volatility that we saw was astonishing.

Advantages

There are usually no trade size minimums, in contrast to trading stocks, commodities, or spot forex. You can also short sell, therefore an up or a down market are both okay with you. Other advantages are that you have the ability to trade directly with the exchanges, brokers are not mandatory. You can trade 24/7 which is even more trading hours than spot forex. Obviously, the liquidity is not equal throughout the day, some times of the day are more liquid than others.

Day Trading

Day trade with caution! For now you are trading mostly against inexperienced traders, but the scene is changing. The autumn of 2017 saw the launch of Europe's first Bitcoin mutual fund in France. There are also reports of several hedge and private funds with huge resources prepping to enter the market.

Market Timing

Getting in at the "perfect time" with Bitcoin and cryptocurrencies is unrealistic. What is going on, weekly double digits gains, is not supposed to, but it is. Using strictly technical analysis or fundamentals will fail you. Look to buy on panic drops, bounces upwards after Bitcoin panic drops have been very profitable. One tactic to deal with the volatility is to have price alerts set for noticeable price moves. I strongly suggest that you accumulate gradually, cryptocurrency wealth takes time. Ignore, as much as possible, the Wild West hype going on. If your crypto position has a 100% + move up, take some profits. If you did not have an existing position, after a major breakout upwards, buy on the pullbacks. The best opportunities are there for the informed and less emotional. This is especially true in an arena with crypto traders who are untested with facing 40-50% drops.

Leverage

Leverage? Use with caution and only with entities that offer reliable stop losses. Bitcoin and cryptos in general, are assets that can move 20-30% (either direction) on some days, therefore your account can easily blow up. You lose money when you get taken out, and that can easily happen with high leverage. Bottom line, stay in the game and any long-term shorting is with extreme caution...keep in mind all the "deaths" of Bitcoin.

Trading Alternate Currencies (Altcoins) & ICOs

- **Alternate Currencies (Altcoins)** The many alternative currencies that have sprung up based off of the idea and/or basic code of Bitcoin.

- **Initial Coin Offering** (ICO) is a way of crowdfunding via cryptocurrency. **ICOs** sell a right of ownership or royalties to a project. A coin in an ICO is a symbol of ownership interest in an enterprise, a digital "certificate". Often confused with a **'token sale'** which refers to selling participation in an economy, giving investors access to the features of a project at a later date.

Before Trading or Investing, Keep in Mind

Many altcoins are useless, the early internet (.com) days all over again. Unfortunately, the scene is currently filled with swindlers and scammers eager to swindle those in the hunt for "overnight" riches. How to navigate the minefield? Search for the biggest gainers, go where the action is, BUT those gains need to backed up with trading volume. The altcoin volume needs to be 500,000 USD+ (for liquidity). The ICO needs a good value/selling proposition. What is the point of the coin? What problem does it solve? The backing team also needs to be top notch.

One of the more successful ICO's was Ethereum, they raised money with a token sale in 2014. In 2017 at least 90 Initial Coin

Offerings have taken place raising 1 billion+ US Dollars. As of December 2017, there were also over 1,200 digital currencies.

Keep in mind with ICO's no one knows for sure which one will take off. If you invest in 5, there is a very good chance 3 to 4 will fail. But the one that does take off returns 10x or more. 10x means that if you invested $10mm, you generate $100mm in total when you sell.

A little tip: with ICO's or basic transactions, send fractions of payment to test transfers. Practice sending .001 for first few transactions, you can go out to 8 decimal places with Bitcoin.

You should be aware that many of the recent venture capital backed ventures have not brought their products to market as yet. In addition, the full uses of BTC and altcoins are just being explored. Many believe, with good reasons, that Bitcoin will be surpassed in value by another coin. Their basis is that rarely in technology does the first mover remain the dominant player after 5-10 years. Bottom line, we are in the early, early days of digital currencies.

SPOTTING THE ICO SCAMMERS!

Some of the best warning signs that you are dealing with scammers.

- Reaching them is difficult. The phone numbers they have can't be found by a simple web search
- The whitepaper is usually short (under 10 pages), filled with basic grammar or spelling errors
- The quality of the website is low or they used some free service to build it
- Their "about us" and registration details are questionable or missing
- The CEO or advisors can't be found on LinkedIn or other professional channels

CHAPTER 32:
What to Expect in The Near Future

I purposely used what to expect in the near future, because making any long-term claims about cryptos is a fool's errand in my view.

Less ICO Madness

The ICO madness will lose some of the irrational gold rush mentality and we will see improved self-policing from the current players in the market. The public and government regulators do have limits on what they will tolerate.

Relevant Regulations

Trading in Bitcoin and other cryptocurrencies remains mostly unregulated. I was recently made aware of the amount of agencies that claim jurisdiction over cryptocurrencies. This is just in the United States alone, you have the Treasury Department's FinCEN, the Securities and Exchange Commission, and the Internal Revenue Service (IRS). The story gets more bizarre, because there isn't even agreement among the regulators on what a Bitcoin is. For example, the IRS treats it as property and the Commodity Futures Trading Commission says it is a commodity. For market participants this bring confusion to new levels. Even with the confusion, to increase the trust of the broader retail and institutional markets, there is a need of more appropriate regulations for this growing market. This should also include swift and robust punishment for those engaging in misconduct.

Waiting to see more of

What I am eagerly awaiting to see more of in the near crypto future.

1-Exchanges will upgrade both security and their capacity to deal with demand surges. Even though crypto exchanges are not subjected to the same level of scrutiny as traditional exchanges, going forward this security issue will become increasingly difficult to keep talking around. Why? the crypto landscape has enough sad tales of hackings with millions being stolen. No region in the world gets to point fingers. It happens in the East and it also happens in the West, to both big and small exchanges. In contrast to funds in your local bank, if your account is hacked at an exchange, there is very little recourse to recovering your funds and as of this writing there is no insurance available. Everyone knows hackers are on a dedicated hunt after cryptocurrency accounts, therefore the defense needs to step up. The internal threats are another set of headaches, they range from insider trading to other financial misconduct from employees.

Several of the regulated and larger exchanges buckled under demand for new accounts during the recent market explosions. They will get a pass this time around, but how many more times will the public or those in power remain so forgiving?

2- Autumn 2017 saw the launch of Bitcoin futures and it will be interesting to see how this plays out. The public has been asking for a more regulated market, well trading on a futures exchange is all about regulations. This is also the first time that Bitcoin traders can hedge their position in a regulated market. They can now take the other side in the market, by shorting.

3- More coins that eliminates the need for miners. Currently, the majority of Bitcoin mining is done by a handful of firms. Not a market healthy situation as they can use this influence in undesirable ways.

4-Improvements in the speed of transactions seems to be catching the attention of many industry influencers. Even for Bitcoin fans, the relatively slow pace of a routine transaction can be an issue. There are several cryptos that are taking on these challenges and I'm excited to see how their stories develop.

Bitcoin and cryptocurrencies have travelled far from the days of when they were mostly associated with criminals. Now there is both a broader and more positive public awareness. Bitcoin futures transactions are even cleared by top name Wall Street firms, something, that not along ago would have been laughed at. For progress to continue as I have laid out, there needs to be less hype, relevant regulations, and greater security plus transparency from the exchanges. These suggestions I believe will secure that cryptocurrencies, as an asset class, moves beyond the early adopters phase.

CONCLUSION

Thank you for making it through to the end of *Asset Class Mastery.* Let's hope it was informative and able to provide you with the first set of tools that you need to achieve your goals of trading and making money.

The next step is to test your skills at trading and build up your risk capital so that you can make additional trades. This will give you the motivation that you need to succeed.

I have several other books on different aspects of trading and asset classes please check them out!

PROFILE OF THE AUTHOR

W**ayne Walker** is the director of a global capital markets education and consulting firm (gcmsonline.info). He has several years experience in leading and coaching teams of Investment Advisors and has managed top performing teams in the Private Client Group based on Bench Mark Earnings (BME).

www.ingramcontent.com/pod-product-compliance
Lightning Source LLC
LaVergne TN
LVHW100310210926
848480LV00003B/1076